Yorkshire

Yorkshire

A Story of Invasion, Uprising and Conflict

Paul C. Levitt

PEN & SWORD
HISTORY

AN IMPRINT OF PEN & SWORD BOOKS LTD.
YORKSHIRE – PHILADELPHIA

First published in Great Britain in 2019 by
Pen & Sword History
An imprint of
Pen & Sword Books Ltd
Yorkshire - Philadelphia

ISBN 978 1 52675 255 0

A CIP catalogue record for this book is
available from the British Library.

Printed and bound in England
By TJ International Ltd.

Pen & Sword Books Ltd incorporates the Imprints of Pen & Sword Books
Archaeology, Atlas, Aviation, Battleground, Discovery, Family History, History,
Maritime, Military, Naval, Politics, Railways, Select, Transport, True Crime,
Fiction, Frontline Books, Leo Cooper, Praetorian Press, Seaforth Publishing,
Wharncliffe and White Owl.

For a complete list of Pen & Sword titles please contact

PEN & SWORD BOOKS LIMITED
47 Church Street, Barnsley, South Yorkshire, S70 2AS, England
E-mail: enquiries@pen-and-sword.co.uk
Website: www.pen-and-sword.co.uk

or

PEN AND SWORD BOOKS
1950 Lawrence Rd, Havertown, PA 19083, USA
E-mail: uspen-and-sword@casematepublishers.com
Website: www.penandswordbooks.com

Contents

Preface

Throw open any book on English history and Yorkshire will inevitably be mentioned. Kings of England came here on their way to conduct military campaigns against the Scots and to put down rebellions and punish unruly barons. They came to York – the most important city in the north of the country since Roman times – to sign treaties and perform other royal duties. But in earlier times, invaders came because they prized the fertile land that later became Yorkshire. Some arrived to plunder what riches they could find and extort huge payments in silver that rulers were ill placed to afford. Others came to conquer and rule over the land until they too became part of it. This is a story about Yorkshire and the people who came here throughout the ages. Many would settle and become our ancestors.

While writing this book, a pattern emerged that suggested a different title from the one originally intended. And so the working title of 'Yorkshire – A Journey Through Time' was changed to what you now see. It suggests a past punctuated by wars, upheaval and revolts – most of which were put down with violence. This may seem a little exaggerated and unfair at first, but in his much acclaimed work, 'The Ascent of Man', the British mathematician, historian and author, Jacob Bronowski, offered a plausible explanation, namely, that the greater the distance between a people and government, or centre of power, the greater the chance that things would fall apart. This had been the chief cause of the collapse of vast and mighty empires throughout history, he pointed out. Bronowski, who lectured at University College Hull, went on to say that the distance between the above entities could only be closed if knowledge resides in the homes and heads of people with no ambition to control others, as opposed to residing in the isolated seats of power. Were these principles at work in a Yorkshire that was – by the standards of the past – greatly removed from the seat of central government and power? Is this why military intervention in the north was inevitable at some stage in history?

Another pertinent observation made by Bronowski was that history itself is not simply a sequence of events that occur, but rather the actions of people. Not just people remembering their past, but people acting and living the past in the present. He held that history is the instant act of decision that crystallises all the knowledge that has been learned since man began. So, using the notion that Yorkshire people merely did what they and their forefathers had been pre-programmed to do, including rebelling against any and every form of authority that was not home-grown, brings me to another interesting point. A term still uttered in these parts is 'Yorkshire grit'. Surely this term arose for a reason? In my long experience I have never heard anyone talk about any other kind of grit and wondered how long the term had been in use. I was mildly surprised to find that 'grit' as a personality trait is a whole area of study in the field of psychology and has been since at least 1892. It seems the qualities it suggests, namely, those akin to spirit, firmness of character, pluck, hardiness, resilience, persistence, tenacity – call it what you will – have been valued at least since the time of the Greek philosopher Aristotle (384–322 BC). It even turns out that 'grit' is a better predictor of achievement than IQ because grit helps to overcome challenges and setbacks (Duckworth 2007). Interestingly, a large study of twins measuring both conscientiousness and grit found that they had a genetic correlation (Rimfeld et al 2016). It is not surprising that this theory is contentious and the research and arguments will continue, but I for one think it feasible that 'grit' is something that is impressed upon people from an early age by parents who themselves faced adversity in various ways. Thus this notion of 'grittiness' and attitude to life may have been passed down from generation to generation up to the present day. Considering Yorkshire's turbulent history, it also seems reasonable to assume that this might indeed be how the term originated. Grit certainly now appears to be recognised by the scientific community as an equaliser that acts as a driving force to override any other potential inequalities. And I would not discount it as being linked in some way to Yorkshire's challenging past.

Acknowledgements

As with my previous book titled Yorkshire's Secret Castles, I am indebted to my talented artist friend, Andreas Renou, for reuse of his impression of the early Norman earth and timber fortress at Skipsea. My gratitude is also extended to Dennis Bromage, whose landscape images grace both the cover and the inside pages of this book. Furthermore, I would like to thank BAE Systems for kind permission to use the Blackburn B2 and Buccaneer photographs. My friend and fellow author Phil Arnott receives a special mention because it was during the many angling trips of our youth that I began to appreciate the truly wonderful countryside on my own doorstep. And once again it would be remiss of me not to mention my wife, who has been a constant source of encouragement while working on this latest book.

Introduction

Travel down the Yorkshire coast from the northeast of the county and the rugged cliffs gently give way to the sandy shores of Holderness, terminating at a peninsula of shingle and sand where the mighty River Humber meets the North Sea. The scene is peaceful enough today, but peer into the past and you will discover a much different story. The majestic yet sometimes daunting Pennine Hills in the west have always had an air of solitude and foreboding. They were feared in ancient times because it was usually from here that fierce Picts and Scots would emerge to kill and plunder. Reason enough for the Romans, arguably the mightiest military force to have landed on our shores, to build forts at strategic points through the Pennines to counter the threat of invasion. To the east of them lies the more forgiving landscape of the Yorkshire Dales, which merges with the Vale of York where the land becomes even richer and more fertile. Here the land was highly prized by the first settlers. Navigable rivers meant that invaders could penetrate and explore deep into the land and build encampments, such as at York, where a mighty Roman fortress once stood. The Romans stayed until the beginning of the fifth century AD and York would remain central to Yorkshire's story throughout history.

As much as the Romans influenced our culture and life in general, they weren't the first invaders to leave their mark and wouldn't be the last. The North Sea became a thoroughfare for traders and invaders. The Celts were among the first to cross it and trade with the indigenous Britons. Later on Angles, Saxons and Vikings all sailed down the Humber with more serious intent. But people were arriving in Yorkshire long before any of these. Human activity in Yorkshire dates back at least 13,000 years to the time when early hunters stalked animals that migrated northwards when the ice retreated. Evidence of their presence and that of subsequent early occupiers has been found here and it was largely thanks to inquisitive landowners exploring the earthworks on their land and in some cases hoping to find treasure that an early picture of the county's occupation over the centuries was obtained. Likewise, other enthusiasts, such as local churchmen, doctors and country squires pursuing their part-time interests, helped to increase our knowledge of the past. And it is fortunate that they did. In the early eighteenth century, one such person expressed his shock at the needless manner by which the grandeur of Roman Britain was heedlessly being destroyed. William Stukeley (1687–1765) was a doctor and by far the most remarkable field antiquary of his day. Another was William Greenwell (1820–1918), a Church of England canon, who together with J.R. Mortimer (1825–1911), a corn merchant from Driffield in the East Riding, excavated many notable barrows on the Yorkshire Wolds, including those at Duggleby Howe and Danes Graves. The canon's work, *British Barrows* (1877), marked a big step forward in British field archaeology and he was among the first to realise the importance of pottery in the dating of sites (Hawkes 1986). Their work made an important contribution to British prehistoric archaeology and the Mortimer Collection, which includes both prehistoric and medieval finds, can be found in Hull at The Hull and East Riding Museum.

We learn much of what occurred in the early years of the Roman occupation from the writings of people such as the great Roman senator and historian, Publius Cornelius Tacitus, who was the governor of Britain from AD 78 to 85. Tacitus, who was born during the emperor Nero's reign and lived at least until the end of Trajan's and possibly Hadrian's reign, was one of the best-known orators of his day and produced two principal historical works, namely, the *Histories* and the *Annals of Imperial Rome*. The latter only survived by a slim chance and lay unappreciated for almost 1,400 years. It wasn't until ancient history became a popular field for translation that it was rediscovered among medieval manuscripts, the first complete edition of his surviving works being published in 1515 (Grant 1956). At the time of the Roman invasion of Britain, Yorkshire was simply part of a tribal territory called Brigantia, a swathe of land stretching across the entire north of England. Having reached terms with the Romans in AD 43, its leaders had been willing to live in peace, but after a quarter of a century of Roman domination, the Brigantes tribe became restless. We recount the exploits of the Romans in Yorkshire right up to the Roman evacuation of the province in AD 410.

The story of Yorkshire continues through the establishment of the Anglo-Saxon kingdoms in England to the near destruction of them by the Danes. The Angles inexorably drove the ancient British tribesmen from the eastern parts of the country to the north beyond Hadrian's Wall and into the Welsh uplands to the west. But they too would be harassed and then terrorised and held to ransom by the Danes. This period was first recorded by the monk, Gildas, in his work, *De excidio et conquestu Britanniae* (The Overthrow and Conquest of Britain) and it wasn't until the late ninth century that unknown clerics compiled the Anglo-Saxon Chronicles, drawing on the earlier sources, such as the Venerable Bede's Ecclesiastical History of the English Nation. Bede personally witnessed England's earliest years and was the first to use the word 'Angle-land'. Most chroniclers came from the ranks of the clergy, who until the thirteenth century were among the few who could read and write. Archdeacon Henry of Huntingdon in his twelfth-century *Historia Anglorum*, used Bede and others as his source. In the early thirteenth century, Gervase, a monk of Canterbury, and Ralph, abbot of Coggeshall, both wrote about the English people and monarchy, as did an anonymous monk at Barnwell Priory in Cambridgeshire. At least one chronicler is known to have Yorkshire connections, namely, Roger of Hovenden, or Howden in the East Riding. He produced a work on Henry II and Richard I, titled *Gesta Henrici II et Gesta Regis Ricardi* (The Chronicle of the Reigns of Henry II and Richard I). When work started on the chronicles, England was a land of many kingdoms and when they had finished, it was united under a single ruler.

During Norman rule the county was turned into one vast military camp with 60,000 knights and many more common soldiers holding their land directly from the king. Feudalism meant that the Norman barons were given land for their loyalty to the new king who could call upon them to render military services at any time during their lives. But the full obedience of the kingdom would take many years to achieve and the Norman landowners built castles to protect their lives and their property. In Yorkshire there are upwards of seventy-five sites where timber and earth castles were erected, some of which were developed in stone. William the Conqueror himself also faced disobedience by his own greedy barons. He addressed this minor inconvenience by merely distributing their lands across many different counties so that it would be difficult for any of them to concentrate their power. This also enabled all of the law courts to be dependent on the crown. In Saxon times an Englishman held land in his own right and chose his own aldermen, who in turn chose the king. After the Norman Conquest this had all been reversed, but eventually Normans and Saxons would intermarry and the population blend into one nation of English. The monarchy would learn to cope with the northern barons and they, in turn, would learn how to deal with the king, their people and perhaps the most difficult of all, with each other. But underlying resentment would lead to conflict throughout the Middle Ages.

In the period known as The Anarchy, which occurred during the reign of Stephen (1135 to 1153), the Scots, under King David I, invaded the north of England, both immediately after Stephen's crowning in December 1135 and again in the spring of both 1137 and 1138. The invasion was intended both to consolidate David's position as king of Scotland, as well as to further his family's interests. Having swept everything before him in Northumberland, he entered Yorkshire expecting the same outcome. But he would be disappointed. Word had gone around about the unbridled and wanton violence of his army, especially the wild, half-naked warriors who had earned a fearsome reputation for their depraved behaviour. This provoked widespread resentment and resistance among the normally quarrelsome Yorkshire barony, who responded by uniting their forces under the banners of their patron saints. Their smaller force confronted the formidable Scottish army at Northallerton and won an unlikely victory in August 1138 at the Battle of the Standard.

Upheaval in Yorkshire would begin anew during the reign of Richard II (1377 to 1400), the last of the Angevin kings, when the seeds were sown for the struggle for the crown that famously became known as the Wars of the Roses, or the Cousins' War. It would span the reign of seven English kings, with the first battle taking place in 1455. But the years from 1460 to 1487 were crucial: the crown changed hands no less than six times within the space of twenty-five years and half of the nobility of England were slain in the battles that took place. Inequalities of wealth towards the end of the fifteenth century were reflected in Robin Hood ballads, which prevailed at that time, but nothing would focus the grievances of Yorkshire people more than the unjust way in which monks had been turned out of monasteries and their goods simply stolen during the reign of Henry VIII. The barbaric and unwarranted execution of innocent church leaders, one of whom came from Yorkshire, exacerbated the situation and in 1536 many thousands rose up in protest. Known as the Pilgrimage of Grace, the unrest would end in the execution of its leaders, as well as four monastic leaders.

Just over a century later, civil war would divide the nation. Irrespective of commonalities, such as wealth and background, the families of gentry would take different sides. Unlike London and the eastern counties, loyalty in the north was inclined towards King Charles I and it was in that direction that he would turn to gather support at the start of the conflict. But a rude awakening would come on reaching Hull in East Yorkshire, the magazine of the north, where Charles had expected the gates to be thrown wide open to receive him. They weren't, and the first pitched battle of unbridled warfare between Royalists and Parliamentarians would take place in October 1642. Barely two years later the Royalist cause in the north would effectively come to an end at the battle of Marston Moor.

In the mid-eighteenth century, Yorkshire was again plunged into conflict when all able-bodied men between the ages of 18 and 50 were ordered to abandon their work and families while they served in the militia for up to three years. This startling and unreasonable piece of legislation caused uproar throughout the shire, especially in the East Riding, which in 1757 experienced its most serious period of unrest since the Pilgrimage of Grace. The riots spread to North Yorkshire and the following year the ringleaders were found guilty of treason at York Assizes. Anti-government sentiments were often dealt with extremely harshly, but surprisingly, only one person was executed on this occasion. This was not the case for sixteen Luddites who were found guilty in York for their part in an outbreak of violence in 1812 and were hanged.

The enemy would come dangerously close to Yorkshire's shores in December 1914 when the German Navy shelled a number of ports in the northeast. Among the most prominent buildings hit during the bombardment was the Grand Hotel in Scarborough and Whitby Abbey. The eventual horror of the First World War was experienced first hand by J.B. Priestley, the Bradford-born novelist and playwright, who saw active service in France and was badly wounded by mortar fire. He fell victim to a gas attack but recovered and would help to maintain the nation's morale during the Second World War through a regular Sunday-night radio slot that attracted millions of listeners to the BBC. In the months following the evacuation at Dunkirk, only Winston Churchill was a more popular broadcaster.

Finally, we should not forget that throughout history Yorkshire has been under constant threat from a force of nature that has claimed a huge swathe of land from the East Yorkshire coast. The invasion by the sea has accounted for more than thirty towns and villages between Flamborough Head and Spurn Point since Roman times and the alarming erosion of Yorkshire's coast seems unstoppable.

Let us now travel far back in time beyond recorded history and imagine a place that would eventually become Yorkshire – where much of England's long and eventful history took place.

Chapter 1

Prehistoric Cultures

Our story begins long before the boundaries of England's historic counties were drawn or even contemplated. Developments took place thousands of years ago that would leave the varied landscape that became Yorkshire. Pollen evidence suggests that the county was once a densely forested region, but repeated encroachment by ice sheets replaced forest with tundra, and it was only during interglacial periods that vegetation would flourish and attract life. About thirteen long and cold periods have been identified over the past 1 million years, the earliest occurring some 450,00 years ago and the latest 18,000 to 13,000 years ago (Penny et al. 1969, Beckett 1981). Ice from this latter period came from the Lake District and southwest Scotland, crossing the Pennines between the Vale of Eden and Teesdale. It also flowed from the northeast, passing either side of the Cleveland Hills and reached a depth of at least 60 metres at the coast, where the North Sea was 160 metres below its present level (Catt 1990). A huge volume of water, known as Lake Humber, occupied the Vale of York and was partially covered by a glacier extending southwards as far as Doncaster and the Isle of Axholm (Gaunt 1976). Deposits visible in the Vale of York and the Wolds escarpment show that the lake reached a depth of 30 metres at one stage. When it had completely drained, we were left with the same river system that today feeds into the Vale of York. Together with the River Trent outfall, this river system flows into the River Humber, which drains one fifth of England's landscape.

If we travel far enough back in time, the climate, flora and fauna were very different from today. Fossilised animal bones found in a cave at a limestone quarry near Kirkbymoorside in 1821 turned out to be no ordinary bones. They were those of long–extinct types of hippopotamus, elephant, bison and hyena, and all were clearly much larger than any of today's species. Kirkdale Cave in the Vale of Pickering is still the most northerly point at which the remains of such species have ever been found and at the time the discovery was nothing short of astounding. Scientific analysis eventually confirmed beyond a doubt that the finds from Kirkdale were between 117,000 and 225,000 years old. In 1837, a similar discovery at Victoria Cave (Fig. 1) in the limestone cliffs near Settle revealed animal bones that were 130,000 years old. Once again these included hippopotamus, woolly rhino, elephant and hyena. Crucially, an 11,000-year-old harpoon point made from reindeer antler turned up during these latter excavations, thus providing the earliest evidence of humans occupying the Yorkshire Dales. Hunters were not supposed to have ventured so far north during the Old Stone Age, even during the warm intervals of the Ice Age (Hawkes 1986).

These and other discoveries pointed towards an ancient climate that oscillated between extremes of temperature. The last ice age peaked some 18,000 years ago when the River Humber was dammed with ice and it would be several thousand years before rising temperatures would enable man to venture further north. During the warm intervals when the ice retreated, the sea level rose to a level where the Yorkshire coastline was much further inland than it is today. Roughly following the perimeter of the Wolds, the chalk cliffs would have stretched inland from Flamborough, through Driffield and Beverley down to North Ferriby on the north bank of the River Humber. In fact, the ancient cliff line crosses the Humber where the Humber Bridge stands today. So, the mouth of the Humber was once 45km further west of Spurn Point (Pethick 1987). This was confirmed when the buried cliff was revealed by road works on the northern approach road to the bridge (Catt 1990). Moreover, the extension of the Humber's length can only have occurred since the present sea level was established 3,000 to 4,000 years ago. A crucial clue to this was obtained from a wood sample found beneath a Bronze Age boat that was discovered in the mud of the Humber estuary (Gaunt and Tooley 1974).

When the ice began to retreat about 15,000 years ago, it created vast lakes, one of which virtually filled the Vale of Pickering, between the Wolds, the Howardian Hills and the North York Moors. Twice as long and many times broader than Lake Windermere, Lake Pickering was first suggested in 1887 and would have easily been England's largest freshwater lake. A clue to the lake's existence lies in the pattern of villages around the vale. What is now the North York Moors once had up to twenty temporary lakes, one of which was home to a community of early hunters who lived on its edge. This was brought to light when, in 1947, an amateur archaeologist found flint artefacts on farmland just to the south of Scarborough and it led to the discovery of a site known as Starr Carr – once a small settlement of around twenty people. Fragile deposits recovered from layers of waterlogged peat proved to be almost 11,000 years old, while further excavations revealed a landing stage for canoes that proved to be the oldest man-made structure in Britain. This platform had stood on birch trees that were cut using stone axes and thus became the earliest known example of trees cut by man. Other highly prized finds were the remains of Britain's earliest house, as well as barbed harpoon points made from antler bone. Perhaps the most astounding find was a decorated shale pendant that is widely regarded as the earliest piece of art ever to be found in Britain.

Warmer temperatures and the disappearance of the ice had enabled trees to grow again, which attracted animals such as deer and wild boar that were hunted by Yorkshire's earliest inhabitants. Food resources were particularly abundant in low-lying areas, which accounts for the richness in sites dating from 7,500 to 4,300 BC in The Vales of York and Pickering, as well as the River Hull valley in Holderness. Evidence of human activity dating back to the early Mesolithic period has been found in the North Riding at Seamer Carr and Flixton, and in the East Riding close to the villages of Kelk, Gransmoor and Barmston. A concentration of finds such as barbed harpoon points made from bone have been discovered around glacial meltwater gravels at Brandesburton and at Gransmoor, while flint implements and flint-working debris have been found in the Vale of York, Holderness and the Hull valley (van der Noort 1996). But another period of glacial activity intervened and the next evidence of woodland clearance occurs in the Yorkshire Wolds area between 8,000 and 9,000 years ago.

It wasn't until the arrival of the first farmers from the continental mainland around 5,000 years ago that major deforestation began. Or so it was thought. New evidence is emerging that has thrown doubt on these earlier assumptions. Recent core samples have shown that dense woodland was cleared by burning down trees 10,000 years ago at up to twenty moorland sites. The evidence suggests that the fires were lit deliberately and the theory goes that the vegetation, which then grew in the absence of trees, attracted grazing animals and thus made them easier to hunt. Manipulating the environment in this way is a foretaste of farming that took place 6,000 years earlier than previously thought.

Evidence of sudden and dramatic climate change has been found in the Yorkshire Dales at White Scar Caves near Ingleton, where 11,000 year old stalagmites formed since the last Ice Age suggest that trees would have struggled to survive in the conditions that prevailed 8,200 years ago. The sudden cooling lasted for more than a hundred years and was followed fifty years later by a violent event, thought to have been a tsunami, that flooded Doggerland and made Britain an island. Neolithic farmers arrived from France 6,000 years ago and had a preference for chalky soils, as found on the Yorkshire Wolds. One thousand years later the area was completely devoid of trees. Evidence of tree felling and differences in land usage comes from fossil pollen grains. In Holderness, the first tree felling took place around 3,900 BC and was being carried out on a large scale by 1,000 BC when arable rather than pastoral farming became the norm. It is argued that the switch from hunting and gathering to farming probably occurred over several centuries, with pioneering farming communities from the continent and hunter-gatherers living side by side. Interestingly, DNA analysis of skeletons has revealed that as little as one in ten of our ancestors belonged to the early continental farming communities, while the vast majority were hunter gatherers (van der Noort 1996). Indeed, the latest research suggests that there may have been quite some resistance to farming and that hunter-gatherers were not as convinced of the need for agriculture as was previously thought. Another interesting theory I heard recently was that warfare only became prevalent after the establishment of agriculture. It was argued that post-agrarian societies, which have existed in various parts of the world for at least 10,000 years, only had reason to fight in defence of their territory when it became an important source of food and therefore wealth.

As more and more land was cleared, Britain's first monuments associated with Neolithic ritual and burial sites started appearing on the landscape. Known as long barrows, these are mainly located on higher ground, such as the Wolds and North York Moors, where two dozen or so have been identified. The largest of these is at Allerston, near Pickering. Built using limestone boulders, it contained cremated human remains and is between 4,500 and 5,000 years old. A long barrow excavated near Scarborough has also produced flint axes, knives and arrowheads. Other examples exist near the villages of Kilham on the Wolds and West Heslerton in the Vale of Pickering where a huge long barrow existed on the wold top. Ploughing and quarrying have taken their toll, but part of the barrow still survives and what started out as a chance discovery during sand and gravel reclamation led to what became one of the largest archaeological excavations in the country. Excavations carried out at Heslerton have revealed evidence of human activity spanning 7,000 years.

Round barrows later appeared on the landscape and would be built until the early and middle Bronze Age. These would become the most common of Yorkshire's prehistoric monuments and often represented burials of high-status individuals. Associated with Beaker Folk who crossed over from the continent about 500 years after the appearance of the first henges, round barrows are more numerous on the Wolds than anywhere else. The Beaker Folk who settled in Yorkshire are thought to have come from the Rhineland area of Germany and were nomadic warriors who were taller and more strongly built than the native population (Hawkes 1986). In 1834, a human skeleton was discovered in a round barrow at Gristhorpe near Filey on the Yorkshire coast. Dating from the Bronze Age, the skeleton was wrapped in a skin cloak and buried in a coffin that was made from a hollowed out oak tree. Grave goods included flint tools and a bronze dagger. When he lived, Gristhorpe Man would have been 6ft tall, an unprecedented height for the Bronze Age. Several healed fractures support the theory that he may have been a warrior as well as a tribal chief. Britain's

best-preserved early Bronze Age skeleton is displayed at the Rotunda
Museum in Scarborough.

A large round-barrow site exists on arable farmland at Arras
Farm on the Wolds escarpment just to the east of Market Weighton.
Centuries of weathering and ploughing has eroded the soil so that
little remains visible above the ground today, but the cemetery once
contained between 100 and 200 small mounds. Dating from the first
millennium BC, the burials included three chariots that had been
previously disassembled. No weapons or pottery were found, but the
discovery gave birth to what is called the Arras culture, which relates
to the Celtic Parisi tribe of pre-Roman Britain. The first Celts are
believed to have arrived in Britain from mainland Europe (Gaul and
the Low Countries) in the fifth century BC, and by the third century
BC they controlled a vast area of Europe. Although they were warriors
who greatly influenced the culture and social structure of Britain,
there is some dispute as to whether their influence was due to invasion
or merely trade, as they arrived in small numbers at various times and
in different regions. However, by the end of the third century their
influence was in decline and their civilisation came to a definitive end
during the course of the Roman occupation.

Round-barrow sites exist at Danes Graves on the Wolds near
Great Driffield and at the villages of Thwing, and Duggleby. It is
estimated that Duggleby Howe (Fig. 2), contains 5,000 tons of chalk
and excavation of the graves there have revealed not only human
skeletons, together with bone and flint objects, but also fifty cremations
from the Beaker period. Perhaps the finest monument to the Arras
culture and one of the best-preserved barrow cemeteries in Britain
can be found at the tiny village of Scorborough near Leconfield in
East Yorkshire. Were it not for the ground in this quiet backwater
never having been under the plough, a cemetery comprising over one
hundred barrows would probably have gone unrecognised. I recall
many years ago fishing for brown trout in the crystal clear waters
of Scorborough Beck, little realising the significance of the land
there in ancient times. Another village on the western fringe of the
Yorkshire Wolds that has a long barrow surrounded by a number of
round barrows is Hanging Grimston. Excavations there have yielded

beakers, urns, human and many animal bones. Barrows also exist in West Yorkshire on the moors between the Rivers Aire and Wharfe.

Chariot burials are also associated with the Arras culture and in 2001, three such burials were discovered in a valley to the north of the village of Wetwang near Great Driffield in East Yorkshire. All of the burials dated from the Iron Age and were of young adults, one of which was female. Grave finds included a polished bronze mirror and a sword and scabbard with bronze decoration. Another exciting grave find close to a chariot burial from the same period was recovered from an Iron Age cemetery at the small village of Kirkburn, which is not far from Wetwang. Excavations in 1987 at the grave of a man in his early twenties to late thirties produced an elaborate sword complete with scabbard dating from 300 to 200 BC. The Kirkburn Sword was described by the British Museum as probably being Europe's finest Iron Age sword.

Henges are mysterious monuments that appear to have no direct connection with burials, but are thought to have been built by ancient Britons to serve as ritualistic landscapes where local groups or tribes met to perform various rites (Hawkes 1986). A fine example can be found on the Yorkshire Wolds and is centred on a 26-tonne monolith dominating the churchyard of All Saints Church in the quiet village of Rudston. At 8 metres in height, Rudston Monolith (Fig. 3) is the tallest prehistoric standing stone in the country. Reputed to be of a similar length underground, the 26-tonne monolith was hauled a distance of 10 miles from Cayton Bay to its current resting place around 4,000 years ago. Forming part of the landscape are four cursuses, or processional avenues, as well as two further henges and four great barrows that lie in or close to the Great Wold Valley carrying the Gypsey Race stream to the sea at Bridlington. Other henge sites can be found near Aysgarth in Wensleydale, near Ripon, and on Sleights Moor near Grosmont, to the southwest of Whitby. Perhaps the most renowned of Yorkshire's standing stones are the 4,000 year old Devil's Arrows (Figs. 4a and 4b), which can be seen from the A1 trunk road just to the west of Boroughbridge. The three huge stones (originally there were at least four and possibly five) were quarried 10 miles away and are arranged roughly in a straight line. Their name is derived from a legend that they were hurled at the church from a nearby hill by the Devil himself. Ilkley Moor also has a series of stone monuments and engravings on flat rock outcrops that are thought to date from the Bronze Age.

Hill forts generally appeared at the beginning of the Iron Age with the gradual spread of the Celtic iron-using culture from Europe. Yorkshire has several hill-fort sites, including those at Almondbury near Huddersfield, Ingleborough in the Yorkshire Dales, and at Danby Rigg on the North York Moors. Others exist at Wincobank in Sheffield, and Carl Wark on the nearby moors. Dating from the end of the Bronze Age, Castle Hill at Almondbury is one of the oldest and largest hill forts in the region. A striking natural landmark that dominates the surrounding countryside, the site was occupied for over 4,000 years and offers spectacular views. Excavations showed that it was burnt down in 430 BC, but became occupied again 1,700 years later by the Normans, who built a motte and bailey castle there. A Victorian tower now stands on the summit. Ingleborough, together with Whernside and Pen-y-ghent, form the famed 'Three Peaks' of the Yorkshire Dales National Park. The summit of Ingleborough is reinforced by a wall built from blocks of millstone grit and is believed to have once been a formidable Brigantian stronghold. Another hill fort associated with the Brigantian tribe is the huge Romano-British Stanwick Camp, near Richmond in North Yorkshire. The latter is featured in the chapter dealing with the Roman period.

The Yorkshire Wolds area is unusually rich in prehistoric earthworks. A network of dykes constructed for protective or defensive purposes may also have been used as cattle drovers' ways. The most formidable example of these is the so-called 'Danes' Dyke' near Bridlington, which was not actually built by the Danes. It stretches the entire width of the Flamborough Head peninsula from coast to coast, effectively cutting it off from the mainland to the west. The dyke is thought to date from the Iron Age, although Bronze Age arrowheads were found there during excavations in 1879.

To the south of Flamborough Head lies Holderness, the relatively flat but rich stretch of agricultural land between the Yorkshire Wolds and the North Sea. Holderness owes its existence to debris, or 'glacial till' that accumulated thousands of years ago along the chalk cliffs of the original coast. Now far inland, the old coast forms the foot of the Wolds area. Once a landscape of lakes and marshes, the entire area now comprises boulder clay, gravel and sand carried from as far away as Scandinavia. The North Sea ice flowed into the area via two different routes and reached inland almost as far as Brough. At Sewerby on the southern side of Flamborough Head, fossils found in the beach shingle at the foot of the cliff indicate that the deposits date from a warm period between 128,000 and 116,000 years ago during the last interglacial (Cat 1990).

Today, coastal erosion is reclaiming the soft deposits of glacial till at a high rate and a strip of land 30 miles long and 7ft wide disappears into the sea each year. I recall the alarming losses from a few acres owned by my father between the cliff-top and the road at Rowlston each winter and was not surprised to read that an estimated 115 square miles of Holderness has disappeared since the Romans invaded Britain (Sheppard 1912). Not far away from Rowlston, melting ice created Hornsea Mere, Yorkshire's largest freshwater lake and the last surviving mere of many that once existed in Holderness. Topographic and place-name evidence suggests that there were upwards of seventy meres that were either drained during the nineteenth century or now lie far out to sea. Peat footprints of those closest to the seashore have occasionally been revealed on the beach following storms, some even with traces of lake dwellings, artificial islands or wooden platforms. One such discovery was made near Withernsea, close to the site of its 'lost' mere. In 1898 the antiquarian, Thomas Sheppard, described how the traces of two dwellings had been exposed on the beach at low water. 'The trunks of trees laid horizontally, showing cuts of the rude axe and the piles with sharpened points binding them together,' he noted. As the relatively soft material of the Holderness cliffs gives way and falls into the sea, other interesting archaeological finds can suddenly turn up on the beach, such as a Neolithic polished flint axe that was found washed from the cliffs. Sheppard also mentions finds from barrows on the shoreline in the Kilnsea area of the Spurn peninsula, which were under continuous threat from the sea in his day.

But the sea did not reclaim all of the Holderness meres. Natural silt deposition and artificial land drainage accounted for some. At Ulrome in 1888, a drainage commissioner who was carrying out work on a major land drain in the area discovered a human skull, oak piles and other wooden structures. It turned out to be evidence of a lake dwelling, the first of its kind to be found in the country. Sheppard left a useful account. 'Mr. Boynton found a large platform measuring 90 x 60ft, held in position within the margin of the lake by oak piles. The lower ones were roughly pointed, principally by burning, and relics of the Stone Age were found.' He went on to describe how a later series of dwellings was built on top of the first during the Bronze Age and how relics, such as a jet bracelet, bronze spearhead and tools made from the sharpened leg bones of oxen, had been found.

In the neighbouring village of Skipsea, lake margin deposits at a former mere have not only revealed man-made wooden platforms, but also evidence of 'heel-coppicing' or deliberate management of a tree to produce timber ideally suited for building or construction. Radiocarbon dating found the samples to be almost 5,000 years old. These finds are among the earliest Neolithic structures found in the British Isles (Gilbertson 1984). Skipsea is even more renowned for a series of earthworks that have been described as the finest of their kind. Dating from the Iron Age, Skipsea Brough comprises a crescent-shaped series of defences that protect the immediate west and southwest of a huge mound that was surrounded by water in earlier times. Stone and bronze implements have been found on the site, including an axe head. Excavations carried out in 2016 confirmed that the earthworks are 2,500 years old and were perhaps built initially as a burial mound. Almost 1,000 years ago the site was chosen again for settlement, this time by the ruling Norman Lord of Holderness, who found it to be the ideal location to build a motte and bailey castle (Fig. 5a and 5b). Despite having once developed a massive stone keep, this has long since disappeared.

Forming the southern boundary of East Yorkshire is the mighty River Humber, which is still today a major transport artery, as it has been through the ages. The ongoing process of silt deposition is gradually reducing the river's width and it has been calculated that over 3 million tonnes of sediment is suspended in its waters at any one time (Pethick 1987). It is this silting that has preserved many artefacts that throw light on the region's past. A most interesting and unexpected archaeological find in this respect was made at Roos Carrs near Withernsea in 1836 when workmen were digging out a ditch; 6ft below the surface they found what appeared to be a model of a boat with a group of human figures. It turned out that the ditch was once a creek feeding the River Humber and it was thought that the model might be the work of early settlers from Scandinavia. The shields carried by some of the figures suggested an earlier period and further analysis showed the carving to be almost 2,500 years old.

One of the most significant marine archaeological discoveries in the country came in 1937 with the finding of an ancient plank boat on the Humber foreshore at North Ferriby. This was followed by the later discovery of a second boat and fragment of a third boat, all of which were dated to between 3,500 and 4,000 years old. More than 16 metres in length and large enough to hold up to eighteen people, the boats had been abandoned on the mudflats of a shallow creek, in what was a well-wooded area at the time. In 1984, what appeared to be a buried tree was found during drain-laying work in a field near Holme-upon-Spalding-Moor, some 13km from the River Humber. It turned out to be an ancient oak tree that had been hollowed out to form a log boat over 12 metres in length. The tree was estimated to have weighed some 28 tonnes and been 800 years old when it was felled approximately 2,300 years ago. The Hasholme boat was found in what was once a tidal creek that joined the Humber between Faxfleet and Brough (Halkon 1990). On closer examination, the wood working skills used in making the boat were among the most advanced seen from the Iron Age in northwest Europe (McGrail 1987).

Chapter 2

The Romans

The earliest recorded history of Brigantia, an area that included a large part of today's Yorkshire, occurs in the writings of the great Roman senator and historian, Publius Cornelius Tacitus (AD 56–117), whose two major works span the history of the Roman Empire from AD 14 to 70. Tacitus was the son-in-law of the real conqueror of Britain, Julius Agricola, who was governor from AD 78. He tells of renewed unrest that occurred some forty years after the Roman invasion of Britain. A tribal territory stretching across the entire north of England from coast to coast, Brigantia had cooperated with the Romans since AD 43. But the Brigantians were endowed with a natural ferocity and firmly believed in the prowess of Caratacus, a guerrilla leader who was previously undefeated in battle and pre-eminent among British chieftains. Any shortcomings in strength they might have had compared with the Romans was more than adequately compensated by his cunning and knowledge of the local topography, or so the British thought. Carrying the war to the even more remote and barren country of the Ordovices in mid-Wales, Caratacus was joined by all of those who wanted to wage war on the hated Romans. Although Caratacus knew it was all or nothing, the British tribesmen were without any kind of armour and were no match for the Romans, either in terms of discipline, training or tactics. They were cut down in what was nothing short of a massacre. Caratacus managed to escape, but his wife and daughter were captured and his brother surrendered. Having sought refuge with Cartimandu, the queen of the Brigantes, Caratacus was entirely at her mercy. But he completely misread where her sympathies lay and he was handed over to the Romans.

In AD 51, Caratacus was sent in chains to Rome. This action would later have unfortunate consequences for the Brigantes. In AD 69 internal divisions within the tribe were a cause of increasing concern to the Romans. Venutius, who was Cartimandu's former husband, had remained loyal to the Romans while married to the tribal queen. But since their divorce he had turned hostile towards her, which caused infighting among the Brigantes. Now ruled by Venutius, the Brigantes tribe would soon face the might of two Roman legions. Cartimandu had been astute enough to gain the upper hand against members of Venutius' family, but this had only added fuel to the fire and she also had enemies who found it unacceptable to be ruled by a woman. The Romans, who had foreseen this eventuality, sent auxiliary battalions to support her. In AD 71, Petillius Cerialis was appointed Roman governor of the province of Britannia and ordered by the emperor Vespasian to quash the revolt once and for all. It was precisely for this purpose that he established a legionary fortress in York. The location lay at a point on the River Ouse that was easily navigable and could be reached by sea-going ships via the River Humber. The newly appointed governor was a highly experienced soldier who had survived defeat at the hands of Boudica, the queen of the Iceni tribe, during a rebellion ten years earlier. He knew much about the land north of the River Humber and set out from Lincoln to establish a military camp at Brough-on-Humber. He would then march to Malton where another camp was established, before turning westwards to York, which became the Roman military headquarters. Soon, the unfortunate Brigantes would be met by not only the Roman legion from York, but also by another Roman legion sent from the west and led by Agricola. Hard pressed on two fronts, the Brigantes chieftain, Venutius, made his last stand in North Yorkshire, where the earthworks at Stanwick Camp can still be seen 8 miles north of Richmond. The fortifications were first built in AD 47 and hastily expanded in AD 72, but the Romans laid siege before they were complete. Encircling the village of Stanwick St John and constituting one of the largest Iron Age settlements in Britain, the ramparts were excavated in 1951–52 by the renowned archaeologist Sir Mortimer Wheeler (1890–1976). He aptly summed up the significance of the site by saying that Stanwick is a very notable memorial to a heroic episode of the British resistance and at the same time a monument to its futility. In clearing a ditch cut by the Brigantes

2,000 years previously, Wheeler used the recovered stones to partially rebuild a small section of wall that can still be viewed today, except that the original wall would have stood an estimated 15ft tall. Finds from the site include an Iron Age sword and wooden scabbard and a human skull complete with sword or axe marks. In 1845, a large number of metal artefacts were found only half a mile away from the site, including a horse mask and horse harnesses for chariots. Dating from the first century AD, the features of the stylised horse mask are typical of Celtic art for that period.

Much as the Normans would do 1,000 year later, the Romans lost no time in building earth and timber forts to establish themselves in the territories they had wrested from the Brigantes tribe. Traces of these forts still exist at Aldborough (near Boroughbridge), Bainbridge, Bowes, Castleshaw, Catterick, Elslack (near Skipton), Greta Bridge, Ilkley, Lease Rigg (near Grosmont), Malton and York. There were also forts at Castleford, Carkin Moor (near Scotch Corner), Doncaster, Newton Kyme (near Tadcaster), Slack (4 miles west of Huddersfield) and at Templebrough (in the suburbs of Rotherham), but there are sadly no ruins visible at any of these. Remains of the fort at Doncaster (Danum) possibly lie under St George's Minster, next to the River Don, while excavations in Castleford (Legiolium) show that the fort lies under modern town centre. In 1534, the antiquarian John Leland wrote that he saw foundations near the church in Castleford and that he thought these could possibly belong to the Roman fort. Crop marks on aerial photographs taken in 1977 also show what appears to be more than one Roman fort at Burghwallis between Castleford and Doncaster. In East Yorkshire, which in Roman times was an area that belonged to the Parisi tribe, a Roman fort existed at Brough-on-Humber (Petuaria). This was a vital staging post for the Romans between Lincoln and York, and since the Romans had been in occupation of Lincolnshire for some thirty years previously, a Romano-British village may even have already existed here before the annexation of what became Yorkshire. In any event, Brough was drastically reshaped along Roman lines around AD 100 and eventually fine stonewalls and buildings were built there. A masonry inscription was discovered that indicates it even had a theatre at some stage between AD 138 and 161.

Occupied until the end of the Roman period, it is probable that the Roman ruins were plundered for dressed stone to build defences at Kingston-Upon-Hull in the fourteenth century (Kitson Clark 1939).

Aldborough, or Isurium Brigantum to the Romans, was the regional capital of the Brigantes and developed into a small walled town in the early second century AD. Rebuilding work, including the defences, was carried out in the fourth century, but the town was abandoned in the fifth century. Today it mainly lies beneath the village, but sections of the outer-wall remain visible, as do fragments of the northern gate. Mosaics have also survived, some of which can be viewed in the adjacent museum. The village of Bainbridge (Virosidum) lies in Wensleydale on a hill at the confluence of two rivers just off the main road (A684) between Leyburn and Sedbergh. Built by Agricola, it was a lonely outpost situated deep in the Pennines. Occupied from the first to the fourth century AD, it was attacked several times and was later expanded with an additional barracks. Like York and many other forts, it was eventually rebuilt in stone. Only its grassy rectangular platform now remains visible. Bowes (Lavatrae) lies to the southwest of Barnard Castle and the fort there stood sentinel on a hill at the eastern approach to the Stainmore Pass, which was the main route used by the Romans to reach Hadrian's Wall to the north. Partially covered by the modern village, the fort enclosure was later chosen as the site of a medieval castle, the remains of which can be seen today. The remote outpost of Castleshaw fort lies at the western extremity of the county and can be found on remote Pennine moorland between Huddersfield and Oldham. The fort was constructed in AD 79, but was only occupied for around 40 years. The site is not large, but the earthwork is clearly defined and its location offers fine views over the valley below. The fort at Greta Bridge, in the historic county of North Yorkshire to the southeast of Barnard Castle, stands where a former Roman road (now the A66 trunk road) crosses the River Greta. The fort was occupied from the second to the fourth century AD and the site and its environs have yielded inscribed masonry, including altar stones, gravestones and a milestone from the Roman period. The earthwork remains can be found behind the Morrit Arms Hotel. Ilkley fort stood on high ground above the River Wharfe and largely lies buried in the town centre beneath All Saints Parish Church and Ilkley Manor House. It dates from the late first century AD and was occupied until the end of the fourth century. Part of the outer defences can still be seen behind the old Manor House, which at the time of writing was an art gallery and museum.

The fort at Malton (Derventio) was built in AD 79 and is the only permanently manned fort known to have existed in East Yorkshire. Attacked several times, it was strengthened in stone twenty years after it was built. Its strategic location within striking distance of the coastal signal stations was reason enough for a cavalry unit to be based there in the fourth century AD. Only a few traces of the ramparts are now visible, but there are several other Roman sites in relatively close proximity to the town. Vestiges of Cawthorn Camps, where Roman soldiers practised their building skills, can be found on the southern edge of the North York Moors, due north of Malton. The well-preserved outlines of no less than four camps, which may indeed have been permanently manned at some stage between AD 90 and 110, exist in this lonely spot.

By far the most important legionary barracks of the Roman army in Brigantia was at York, or Eboracum. Built initially to house the 9th Legion, around 6,000 troops were permanently stationed there from AD 71. The garrison was strengthened between AD 79 and 85, and was rebuilt in stone around AD 107. When the emperor Hadrian came to Britain in AD 122, he brought with him the 6th Legion to replace the 9th Legion, which would remain in York until the end of the Roman era. Despite the strengthening of defences in the north and the building of Hadrian's Wall, which was completed in AD 138, Hadrian's successor, Antonius Pius, had ambitions to expand the empire further north, for which he built the Antonine Wall. But pushing forward the lines of defence resulted in the stretching of manpower, during which Roman forts came under renewed attack midway through the second century AD. A decision in AD 196 to pull out Roman troops from the north to support the fight against the Gauls merely left Brigantia wide open to assault from hostile northern tribes. The situation was saved in AD 208 when the emperor Septimius Severus came to York late in his reign and set up the imperial court from which he would rule the entire Roman Empire. As the nearest legionary fortress to the northern frontier, York was used as a springboard to retake the Antonine Wall and also to strengthen Hadrian's Wall. However, in late AD 210, when the Roman Empire was at its peak, the emperor suddenly fell ill and died shortly after in York, aged 65. By the third century AD York comprised not just a stone-built military fortress on one bank of the Ouse, but also a walled, first-rank town or colonia on the opposite bank. As capital of the Province of Britannia Inferior, York was now well connected by roads built to Roman standards in all directions.

Brigantia enjoyed relative peace during the third century, but towards its end the Saxons started raiding Britain's east coast. To make matters worse, in AD 286 civil war broke out among the Romans themselves, during which northern tribes took the opportunity to raid the forts south of Hadrian's Wall. It required the intervention of the emperor Constantius I to restore the status quo and undertake the necessary restoration work, which included strengthening of the defences at York. He died there in AD 306 and his son was proclaimed the new emperor. By the early fourth century, peace was restored and the fortifications at York had reached their maximum extent. Today, the western multi-angular tower, which dates from this period, can still be seen in the gardens of the Yorkshire Museum, along with a section of the original Roman south-west stone wall, which in the fourth century overlooked the River Ouse. The rectangular east corner tower also survives and is best viewed from the city wall walkway (Fig. 6), where it can be seen below the medieval wall. Other surviving sections of the original Roman wall exist near Monk Bar and near the theatre in St Leonards' Place gardens. The most obvious relic on view from the Roman period can be seen opposite York Minster, where a 9.5 metres high column has been erected. It was found in 1969 underneath the minster during a project to strengthen the foundations. Other interesting discoveries that were made are on view in the minster's under-croft, as well as in the Treasurer's House. Sadly, no visible remains of the colonia exist.

But dark clouds were looming. The Roman soldier and historian, Ammianus Marcellinous (AD 325–400), wrote a chronicle in which he mentions increasing raids by marauders half a century after the restoration under Constantius I. These included Britons, Saxons, Scots, Picts and even Roman deserters, and led to a tumultuous situation in Britain between AD 364 and 369. The lack of an effective military force enabled the marauders to move from place to place looting Roman towns, forts and villas alike. It wasn't until the emperor Valentinian I ordered his leading general, Theodosius, to leave Gaul for Britain that order was fully restored within the province. In addition to repairing the broken Roman defences in Brigantia, a new string of signal stations was constructed, which comprised small forts with wood and stone towers up to 30 metres high. They were built on the North Yorkshire coast from Hunt Cliff near Saltburn to Filey and possibly to Flamborough Head in East Yorkshire, although no trace of the latter has been found. These were all destroyed in the fifth century AD when the Romans effectively left Britain to defend itself, but the best-preserved traces have survived at Goldsborough, 5 miles northwest of Whitby and also at Scarborough. There was also a signal station at Ravenscar to the north of Scarborough, where an inscribed piece of masonry was found in 1774 and is now an exhibit at Whitby museum. It is possible that the line of signal stations extended from Flamborough to Spurn Point at the mouth of the River Humber, but coastal erosion will have long since eradicated any traces of these. Rising sea levels may also have taken their toll, as flooding is known to have occurred in the fourth century, causing abandonment of some Romano-British sites in the Vale of York and along the Humber estuary.

The declaration of intent to withdraw Roman protection made by the emperor Honorius in AD 410 cleared the way for successive waves of invaders to populate the British Isles.

The Roman withdrawal also signalled the beginning of the end for Roman culture on these shores. They had introduced towns with proper paved streets and stone dwellings, and public buildings with amenities such as water supplies, baths, toilets, and drainage, to name a few. In the towns there were shops, markets, workshops, inns, schools, libraries, temples, and even amusements. The residences of noble Brigantians had colourful wall frescoes, fragments of which have survived and can be seen where they were found in Aldborough

(North Riding). Others, for example those found in Catterick, can be seen in the Yorkshire Museum in York. In the countryside, the wealthy Romano-British lived in villas with plastered and decorated walls and mosaic floors, Turkish baths and even central heating. Villas were at the hub of farming estates and were usually not far away from towns such as Aldborough, Brough-on-Humber, Catterick and York. Relatively few villas have been found in the north of England as these fell into decay or were destroyed at the end of the late fifth century. Yorkshire, however, is well represented. Naturally, not everyone lived in a villa or town and poorer inhabitants lived in simple thatched huts that had not changed much since the Iron Age. Such communities have been identified in West Yorkshire around Malham, Ingleborough and Settle, and in Airedale and Calderdale (Garlick 1971).

Other communities from the period have also been discovered close to the banks of the River Humber. In 1967, quarrying work near Brough-on-Humber turned up large quantities of Romano-British pottery, building materials and a lead ingot. Analysis of the pottery recovered from a site between Faxfleet and Broomfleet gave a picture of a settlement having existed there from the late first to fourth centuries AD. Lead was being mined in Yorkshire, Derbyshire and Shropshire during the Roman period and was potentially one of the commodities passing through the site. A large hoard of lead ingots was discovered at Brough in 1940 and a large concentration of Derbyshire ingots found in close proximity to the settlement underlined the importance of the Humber as a trade route with the continent (Bartlett 1968). It is thought that rising sea levels may have ended occupation of the Faxfleet-Broomfleet site, which was originally linked by a creek to the Humber.

With Roman rule having officially ended, the garrisons departed for Gaul and beyond, leaving wealthy Romano-British citizens with no alternative than to try and keep their treasure safe from whoever might invade next. The Anglo-Saxon chroniclers, who were drawing on the writings of The Venerable Bede (AD 673–735), would later record that the Romans took with them to Gaul all of the gold that they could carry and buried the remainder in the earth so that it would never be found.

Chapter 3

Germanic Peoples

Formerly referred to as the Dark Ages and also as the Heptarchy, the period between the establishment of the Anglo-Saxon kingdoms in England (late fifth century AD) and their near destruction by the Danes (ninth century AD) was first recorded by the monk, Gildas, in his work, *De excidio et conquestu Britanniae* (The Overthrow and Conquest of Britain), which provides the only near-contemporary source for history of this period. It was not until the late ninth century that unknown clerics compiled the Anglo-Saxon Chronicles, drawing on the earlier sources, such as the Venerable Bede's *Ecclesiastical History of the English Nation*. At the time they began their work, what we now know as England was a land of many kingdoms. When their work was finished, England was a united kingdom administered by the Normans.

Although the Roman occupation of Britain officially ended in AD 410, the decline of Roman way of life had begun much earlier. A weakening in power and prosperity around AD 350 was followed by the arrival on our shores of Teutonic people – Angles and Saxons – who arrived from across the North Sea in their long ships, exploring the lands along the east coast. One can imagine their sails appearing along the coast and the alarm it raised among the local inhabitants. These new settlers ventured up the River Humber to where the Wolds escarpment meets the foreshore, just west of where the Humber Bridge stands today. Many disembarked there and travelled northward. We know this because of Anglian cemeteries that have been found in villages such as Sancton and North Newbald, both of which lie on the route of the old Roman road that leads north from Brough. Evidence, such as that found in Yorkshire, suggests that large numbers of Anglo-Saxons had already settled in England well before the dates stated in the Anglo–Saxon Chronicles. One such early Anglo–Saxon settlement complete with cemetery was found at West Heslerton, where occupation continued for at least another 400 years. Similar settlements have been identified at York and Rudston on the Wolds, as well as at Driffield, where Aldfrith, king of the Northumbrians, is known to have passed away in AD 705. Settlers would have also continued up the Rivers Trent and Ouse and colonised areas further inland.

Despite the influx of raiders and settlers from the continent, the main threat in the north at this time was from the Picts, who had used the opportunity of Roman withdrawal to scale the two defensive walls built by them in the north. The British had sent men over the sea to Rome to ask for help against the Picts, but after some initial assistance, Rome decided that it had problems enough of its own trying to keep Attila the Hun at bay and their support eventually dried up completely. Help was then sought from the Angles, who in AD 449 were invited by King Vortigern to Britain. They duly arrived in three long ships and in return for fighting the Picts they were granted territory in the southeast. But when the Angles realised just how reliant their hosts were on them for their protection against the Picts, not to mention the choice nature of the land they had been ceded for their trouble, the Angles must have thought that all was for the taking. They sent for reinforcements and, after dealing with Vortigern's enemies, turned on the Britons themselves. In AD 455 there was a showdown between the Angles and the Britons at Aegelesthrep (modern-day Aylesford in Kent), where Horsa, chief of the Angles, was slain. A further confrontation between the Angles and the Britons took place the following year when the latter were routed and forced to abandon Kent for London. The two sides fought continuously for the remainder of the fifth century, but in sixth century there was half a century of relative peace.

York was plundered by the Saxons in AD 504, but the Angles who settled in Yorkshire arrived in or before AD 547, the year that Ida landed at Flamborough Head on the Yorkshire coast with forty vessels and founded the kingdom of Bernicia. Together with Deira, the equivalent of today's Yorkshire, the two kingdoms stretched roughly from a line drawn between the Rivers Humber and Mersey up to the

Forth in Scotland. Originally separated by a tract of forest between the rivers Tyne and Tees, the border between them was later fixed at the Tyne. The progress of the Angles in Deira had been slow, with Ella being the first English king to reign over the kingdom in AD 559–560. But in AD 593, Ida's grandson, the great warrior king, Aethelfrith, became king of Bernicia. A decade later he was also king of Deira. Aethelfrith's success in battle against the Britons greatly expanded the kingdom and it is likely that he destroyed a British army at the battle of Catterick in or around AD 600. In AD 617 Deira was united with Bernicia under Edwin, who became the Bretwalda or Emperor among the kings of Britain. The combined kingdoms were now called Northumbria, which at that time became the mightiest Anglo-Saxon kingdom in Britain. The new kingdom stretched from Hadrian's Wall in the north to the River Humber in the south, and right across the country from the North Sea to what is now the Lancashire coast. Under a succession of strong Northumbrian rulers, the north-British tribes were pushed back into Cumbria, Galloway and Strathclyde. 'Part of the Britons retained possession of Strathclyde and Cumbria, extending from Alcluyd, now called Dunbreton, or Dunbarton – the Dun or fortress of the Britons, to the southern borders of Lancashire, while the ridge of mountains, not inaptly termed the British Apennines, separated them from Northumbria,' wrote Palgrave.

> Though unconquered, they were overshadowed by the supremacy of the Anglo-Saxon sceptre: they bent before the Anglo-Saxon throne, and rendered tribute to the Anglo-Saxon kings. Thus did the dominion of the Britons pass away; thus were the British people either banished from their own country, or reduced into vassalage. And the island from the Pictish sea (Firth of Forth) to the shore of the Channel, became the inheritance of the Anglo-Saxons, who caused their own language, and their own customs and laws, to become paramount in Britain.

In practical terms, the displaced Britons would have simply sought and found shelter beyond the lands that the invaders chose to occupy.

Although the Angles had reached Carlisle, many dependencies of the Cumbrian kingdom extended into modern-day Yorkshire and at one stage, Leeds was the frontier town between the Britons and the Angles, but the former were always giving way. After the destruction of Dunbarton where the British kings usually resided, the displaced Britons became the subjects of the Scottish line that probably acquired its rights by intermarriage with a British princess. They would gradually melt away into the surrounding population, losing their language and ceasing to be discernible as a separate race. Not only that, the Scottish monarchs themselves would later become Saxonised and their ancient subjection become the basis of the supposed feudal rights of Edward I and the primary cause of bloody wars that desolated both countries until the union of the crowns (Palgrave 1876).

Although Christianity had been introduced to our shores during the Roman occupation, it was Pope Gregory I (AD 540–604) who instigated the first recorded large-scale mission to convert the Anglo-Saxons in England to Christianity when he sent Augustine from a priory in Rome to this country in AD 596. The story goes that after seeing slaves for sale in Rome around AD 588, Gregory was particularly struck by the angelic appearance of some boys who had ruddy cheeks, blue eyes and long, fair curls. Long hair among males was a token of dignified birth in those days, as only the privileged classes were entitled to wear their hair long. After enquiring to which nation the boys belonged he was told that they were Angles from Deira. The Anglo-Saxons north of the River Humber resisted conversion to Christianity, but the day would eventually arrive in AD 627 when Edwin, the king of Northumbria, was baptised. Edwin's palace was in what is now the picturesque village of Buttercrambe on the River Derwent. The ancient site at Aldby Park still has traces of a dry moat and Saxon mound where the palace once stood. According to the Venerable Bede, Edwin had survived an assassination attempt at the hands of an ambassador sent by the king of Wessex in AD 625–626. The attack caused Edwin's heavily pregnant wife, Ethelburgha, to go into labour and when the situation became critical, Paulinus, the newly appointed bishop of the Northumbrians, prayed for them. He was a guest in Edwin's household and was awaiting his chance to broach the subject of Edwin's conversion to Christianity when his prayer was answered. Edwin, who in the meantime had recovered from his wounds sustained during the assassination attempt, was about to go to war to punish those who had conspired against him. Although he was hesitant about personally being baptised into Christianity, he pledged to Paulinus that if God helped him to defeat his enemies, he would give his newly born daughter to God and put the question of baptism to the kingdom's elders.

As fate would have it, Edwin was indeed victorious over his enemies in Wessex and therefore kept his pledge to Paulinus. Within twelve months of his daughter's baptism the king and all of his retainers were baptised in York, where a wooden church was built and called St. Peter's. As a further act of gratitude and acknowledgement, Edwin appointed Paulinus Bishop of York and built a larger church, this time of stone. As promised and in keeping with Anglo-Saxon tradition, Edwin had put the matter of whether or not the entire kingdom should adopt Christianity before the elders for debate. They voted to do so unanimously and one of Edwin's most trusted counsellors, the high priest Coifi, even volunteered to personally destroy the heathen temple at Goodmanham, near Market Weighton in the East Riding. Tradition has it that the present church was erected on the original heathen site, which is thought to have also occurred in many other places following the adoption of Christianity. Rudston, where the prehistoric monolith stands today, is such a case in point. When it came to baptising the Northumbrians in AD 628, it took Paulinus thirty-six consecutive days to immerse the eager multitude.

Within a century, Christianity was firmly accepted throughout Anglo-Saxon Britain. Edwin reigned for seventeen years, but in AD 634 he was killed together with his son, Osfrith, in battle against the heathen kings of Mercia and Gwynned (North Wales) at Hatfield Chase near Doncaster in South Yorkshire. The defeat was a setback for Christianity in Northumbria, but during the subsequent reign of Edwin's nephew, Oswald (AD 634–641), Celtic monks from the Isle of Iona came to the area with a view to rekindling Christian belief. These missionaries established monasteries and erected large, intricately carved stone standing-crosses at preaching sites throughout the countryside, such as at Filey and Hunmanby, where Celtic stone-cross fragments have been found (Barley 1939). There is also an ancient and rare eighth-century prayer cross shaft in the churchyard at St Mary's at the picturesque village of Masham in Wensleydale. The badly worn carvings are believed to include depictions of Jesus with the apostles and other figures awaiting baptism. It is thought that the cross might have been erected as a dedication to St Wilfrid, who was the bishop of Ripon from AD 667–669. St Mary's Church itself is of Norman origin, but an earlier Saxon foundation dating from the reign of King Edwin (AD 616–633) stood near this site. Another cross relating to this period can be found at a round barrow thought to be the burial place of Lilla, a nobleman at Edwin's court who allegedly died while saving Edwin's life. Lilla Cross stands at Lilla Howe to the southeast of Grosmont, high on the North York Moors, where fine views extend in all directions.

In AD 664, a significant event occurred when the Synod of Whitby decided that Easter should be held according to the Church of Rome and not according to the Celtic (Ionian) tradition. Christian practice in Northumbria was henceforth changed to align with that of Rome and the episcopal seat moved to York from Lindisfarne where Aidan, the monk from Iona, had founded a Christian community. It was at this time that a hermit called Wilgils, seeking solitude by the sea, chose to found a chapel and monastery near Spurn Point in Holderness. In his account of St Willibrord – the first bishop of Utrecht who brought Christianity to the Frisians, the monk and scholar, Alcuin of York (AD 735–804), mentions how Willibrord's father, Wilgils, came to the promontory and founded a religious community there between circa AD 670 and 770. Similarly, St John of Beverley (died in AD 731) would build a monastery in Beverley, effectively founding the town. Exactly when John was born at Harpham near Driffield in the East Riding is unknown, but he is reputed to have been the son of noble parents and became the Bishop of Hexham and then of York. As a member of the Whitby Christian community, he would have known St Hilda (c. 614–680) and personally have ordained the Venerable Bede both as a deacon and then a priest, a fact recorded by the latter in his ecumenical writings. John was canonised in AD 1037 and the cult that built up around him was a major factor in Beverley's prosperity during the Middle Ages. He was well known for having performed miracles both during his lifetime and after. The King of England, Edward I, is known to have been a devotee and contributed funds for a new and more fitting shrine.

Known as 'The Hammer of the Scots', Edward paused at Beverley Minster (Fig. 7) on his way north to fight campaigns and would always take the banner of St John with him. He would not be the only monarch to use the banner in military campaigns (Palliser 2004). King Henry V attributed his victory at the Battle of Agincourt to the miraculous intervention of John (Gross 1990). The battle, having been fought on 25 October, coincided with the anniversary of John's re-entombment in 1307 (Walsh 2007). Henry, who visited Beverley with Queen Catherine in 1420 to make offerings at John's shrine, ordered the feast of St John to be celebrated throughout England. John's shrine, however, would be destroyed in 1541 during the English Reformation (Palliser 2004). Nothing was heard again until 1664 when workmen discovered a stone vault under the floor of Beverley Minster in which were found ashes, six beads, three great brass pins and four large iron nails – all encased in lead and with an inscription stating that the relics were of the blessed St John and were found and re-interred in 1197. The present floor of Beverley Minster dates from 1738 when relics were again disturbed and an arched brick vault with a marble slab placed over them. A tradition is maintained in Beverley to this day whereby on the Thursday nearest 7 May (St John's feast day) the choir and members of the congregation of Beverley Minster attend evensong at the church of St John of Beverley at Harpham, prior to which they walk in procession to the well, which is decorated with flowers. Another tradition that has been maintained up to the present day is for a procession of civic dignitaries in full regalia to enter Beverley Minster via the great west door (normally closed) on the nearest Sunday to 7 May for a service that is attended by children from Harpham. The children carry primroses gathered from the woods near the village to place around St John's tomb.

A brief word about St Hilda is also appropriate at this point, as she was important in the conversion of Anglo-Saxon England to Christianity. We learn from Bede that she was the daughter of a nephew of Edwin, King of Deira, and was raised at Edwin's court following the death of her father when she was an infant. Hilda would have witnessed Edwin's conversion to Christianity in York, as she herself was baptised as a young girl with other courtiers on the same occasion in AD 627. When Edwin fell in battle against the Mercians at Hatfield Chase near Doncaster in AD 633, Hilda fled with Edwin's queen to Kent, but later returned to the north and became a nun. At first she was planning to join her widowed sister at Chelles Abbey, Paris, but was encouraged by Bishop Aidan of Lindisfarne to return to Northumbria. After a year in a convent somewhere on the north bank of the River Wear, she was appointed the second abbess of Hartlepool Abbey and in AD 657 became the founding abbess of Whitby Abbey (Fig. 8), where she remained until her death. According to Bede, Hilda was a woman of great energy, as well as a skilled administrator and teacher. Her reputation for wisdom brought kings and princes to seek her advice. But she also had a common touch and was called 'mother' by all who knew her.

Despite the inroads made by Christianity, internal feuding was rife among the Anglo-Saxons, especially in Northumbria, which was for a long time the home of literature and religion in England. In his history of the Anglo-Saxons, Sir Francis Palgrave summed up the lack of supremacy attached to royal power with these words:

> As one faction or another prevailed, the kings, who were in truth only the puppets of these factions, were expelled or restored: hailed as monarchs, or slain as traitors and usurpers; and the greater part were of dubious lineage. Among a rude people, who, whether justly or not, considered royal authority as appertaining to a peculiar caste, this defect of ancestry alone was enough to prevent any efficient authority, by depriving the kings of that foundation of opinion, upon which all peaceable dominion is founded.

In his opinion, although the Anglo-Saxons were quite sensible in theory, the first element of government was wanting:

> Peace could never have been ensured in a country where the different subordinate chieftains retained the full right of declaring war against one another. Such petty warfare could not have taken place if the Anglo-Saxon monarchs had possessed that degree of supremacy over their people, which we now consider as an essential attribute of royal power. This loose and imperfect government accustomed the people to strife and dissention and the Anglo-Saxon states were miserably divided by internal feuds.

Chapter 4

The Vikings

However ruthless and ungovernable the Anglo-Saxons were, an even more savage, brutal and warlike force was poised to invade and wrest control from them. In the words of Palgrave, the Danes, Northmen, or Vikings were never at peace and depended wholly on war and plunder. 'From this era, the Danes became the incessant and inveterate foes of Britain and its inhabitants, visiting every part of the island with fire and sword. They are always before us; we always see the horizon reddened with flame, we always hear the tramp of war.' In his *History of England and Great Britain*, Meiklejohn captured the nightmare facing the country when he wrote:

> The miseries and horrors, which the English or Saxons brought upon the British, these the Danes now brought in threefold upon the English. The same terrible sights that had burst upon the panic-stricken eyes of the British, three hundred years before, now amazed the English. The same line of blazing homesteads and corn-ricks against the midnight sky, the same slaughter of priests, women and infants – some of them tossed from spear to spear by the heathen and bloodthirsty worshippers of Woden – and the same levelling of church and palace with the ground.

Throughout the first millennium, the tribes of Europe were taking part in unprecedented levels of migration. The collapse of the Roman Empire released unbridled waves of Huns, Goths and Vandals who moved across Europe displacing native tribes. On the edge of this disturbance was Scandinavia, from where people would come to British shores from the late eighth century until AD 1100 looking for richer land and more space to live. The question arises, when exactly does a 'migration' become an invasion? The Vikings were thought to have left their homelands in Scandinavia initially due to overcrowding and declining resources, but later on their mass migration was equally due to a weakness they perceived in the English. Although they shared similarities and kinship with the Anglo-Saxons, the Vikings viewed them as being weak and cowardly. Their rejection of Valhalla for a new and unfathomable religion was a further reason to despise them, but most of all the heathen Viking chieftains imagined that they had as much a right to rule the Anglian states of Britain as the Anglo-Saxons (Palgrave 1876). This view seems to have been particularly valid for Yorkshire, as Binns wrote in *A Viking Century in East Yorkshire*:

> The very high correlation between family strife in a kingdom and the outburst of Viking raiding in it was not necessarily directed from some operations room by the genius of Ivar the Boneless. It may be that it simply provided a fertile soil in which the ever-present spores of Viking activity could multiply rapidly. This certainly seems to have been the case in Yorkshire; the attraction seems not to have been so much geographic proximity as the absence of a central ruling family whose authority was generally accepted.

Whatever the case may be, the Vikings generally seem to have feared nothing and pitied no one. In AD 789 the first three Viking ships arrived from a region of Norway called Horthaland and unceremoniously killed the reeve who was bold or foolish enough to engage with them and ask what they were doing in those parts. While all of this had been going on in the south, Northumbria, which was first attacked in AD 793, was distracted by struggles of its own, namely, a civil war between rival claimants to the throne. That particular year was not a good one in many other respects. In addition to a great famine in the land, the church in Lindisfarne was sacked and the monks slaughtered by Vikings. Their next recorded act of violence was against the monks in Jarrow, a year later. In the early ninth century, there were repeated forays in the south, but by the middle of that century there was a clear intention to stay. The ultimate demonstration of intent came in AD 851 when 350 heathen ships entered the mouth of the River Thames and caused the greatest carnage ever experienced on our shores up to that point.

The Viking presence in Yorkshire reached a crucial stage in AD 867 when a heathen force, which in AD 865 had been bought-off in the south with a huge bribe or 'Danegeld', now made its way north via East Anglia. Danegeld payments by the English would continue through to the tenth and eleventh centuries. More than 30,000 Anglo-Saxon coins found in great hoards in Sweden bear testimony these payments, which were sometimes recorded on runic memorial stones to Viking warriors. One such stone recorded that, 'Ulv has taken three gelds in England. That was the first that Tosti paid, then Thorkel paid, then Cnut paid,' (Wilson 1970). The heathen force arrived in York on 1 November AD 866 and captured the city on 21 March the following year, from where it staged further carnage and destruction. Although a relief Northumbrian army was assembled, it was no match for the Vikings and the Northumbrian king, Osbert, and a noble usurper called Ella, were killed during the action. The survivors made peace with the Viking force, which was now permanently in the country, but the Vikings were the new masters and appointed the Northumbrian, Egbert, as the vassal king of Bernicia. The ensuing year the Vikings switched their focus to the adjoining kingdom of Mercia. Had the Northumbrians and the Mercians worked together with the West Saxons, their united forces would have been adequate to deal with the Viking threat, but they were too busy contending among themselves to organise any kind of united resistance. Thus the Northumbrians were punished and the Mercians now felt the scourge (Palgrave 1876).

Archaeological investigations carried out in the late 1970s showed that the Vikings had built a large community within the old Roman walls of York. Their wooden houses were uncovered beneath Coppergate and proved to be the first of their kind ever to be found in England. Amazingly, it became evident that the boundaries of the houses and the street plan had scarcely changed in 1,000 years. The Viking houses are preserved in the basement of a shopping complex and visitors can sample the sights and sounds of life how it once was in York at the

Jorvik Viking Centre. Although York clearly suited their purposes, it wasn't the only place the Vikings would settle. Scotland, The Faroe Isles, The Isle of Man, Dublin, Cork and Limerick would all serve as bases for their piratical attacks. And it was the same on the Continent, where virtually the entire western seaboard with its many major river entries invited the attention of the Vikings. In AD 911 they would settle in Normandy and even raid Spain in the mid–ninth century (Wilson 1970). A rare and precious relic of the Viking period is still kept in York Minster, namely an ivory drinking horn that belonged to a nobleman called Ulf who gifted it when he disinherited his sons and granted his lands to the Archbishopric of York. Such symbolic tokens served to impress the event of a transaction upon witnesses and were as important as title deeds and charters (Palgrave 1876).

In AD 869 the Vikings were back in York where they settled the surrounding countryside and farmed the land, gradually becoming Anglo-Danes. With the exception of Wessex they were effectively masters of all England, but there were signs of change. 'Though the Viking army had had not yet been decisively defeated in the field, and had indeed theoretically subdued Mercia and Wessex, it may have been becoming clear that there were no more cheap, easy and lucrative victories to be won,' wrote Binns.

> A large part of the Viking army under Halfdan (Halfdene or Healfdene in Old English) Ragnarsson evidently decided to return to York before things got worse, and it was this group which returned to Yorkshire in AD 874 and the next year began to plough and make a living for themselves in the words of the Chronicle.

In AD 876, Halfdan divided up Northumbria and despite a famous victory over the Danes in AD 878, Alfred, king of Wessex was unable to expel them from Britain. Instead, he was forced to cede extensive territory to them. Today's Yorkshire became part of that territory, which was known as Danelagh or 'Danelaw'. Covering half of England, it comprised a huge swathe of land that stretched from the Tees in the north to the Thames in the south and York was its capital. This Danish kingdom remained independent of England until AD 954, when Eadred the king of Wessex gained a major victory over Eric Bloodaxe in York. It marked the end of Viking domination in Northumbria and was followed by a quarter of a century of peace.

Following Halfdan's death, Ragnald, a Norwegian Viking from Dublin, held sway in York. Although he had accepted Alfred's son, Edward the Elder, as his overlord in AD 920, Ragnald's successor, Sihtric, did nothing of the kind. But Aethelstan (AD 924–940) would soon stamp his authority on Northumbria and the kingdoms beyond, including the kingdoms of the Scots, the West Welsh, and of Gwent. Their respective kings swore their allegiance to him in AD 927 at Eamont Bridge near Penrith, after Aethelstan had driven out Guthfrith, the king of the Dublin Vikings, who had unsuccessfully sought to capture York. All was then relatively quiet for a number of years until AD 934 when Aethelstan was in East Yorkshire facing an impending invasion of the Scots. The invasion finally came in AD 937 when an English army under Aethelstan defeated the Scots and their allies, including Irish Vikings, at Brunanburh. The whereabouts of this key battle remains a mystery to this day, although various locations have been suggested, including Bromborough on the Wirral. Unfortunately, Bromborough does not tally with an ancient account suggesting that the Viking force had travelled a good distance into Aethelstan's kingdom prior to doing battle. This suggests a location somewhere near York, as reasoned by Binns:

> A fleet of 615 ships is said to have collected, which would suggest an army of about 30,000 men. Symeon and Flores say that this fleet entered the Humber, but this has seemed unlikely to some historians, not without reason. It certainly seems strange that forces coming from Dublin should be transported around the north of Scotland instead of landing, as for instance Sihtric had done in 920, on the west coast between the Lake District and Chester, an area familiar to them and inhabited by a Norse population that might have been expected to be sympathetic to their cause. The *Gesta Regum* account of Brunanburh suggests that the Viking forces

had come a good way into Aethelstan's territory before the battle. Although the site has never been identified, this extent of penetration suggests that it was south of York. The use of the Humber by the fleet would then not be as unlikely as it seems at first.

Solving the mystery of Brunanburh's exact location is not entirely without hope and brings to mind the remarkable story of a much older mystery, namely, that of Rome's lost legions. In AD 9, a Roman army led by Publius Quinctilius Varus was completely wiped out by tribesmen in the Teutoberger Forest region of Germany. It was a huge military disaster in which three legions and support troops totalling 20,000 men were annihilated. The unprecedented loss was devastating to imperial Rome, to the extent that Augustus Caesar was reported by the Roman historian Suetonius to have cried out in anguish, 'Quinctilius Varus, give me back my legions!' Hermann, the tribal leader responsible for bringing about the downfall and who was known to the Romans as Arminius, actually commanded German auxiliaries attached to Varus' legions. He knew them intimately, but he was playing a double game that led to him becoming a German legend. The Roman senator and historian, Tacitus, even referred to him as the man who freed Germany. An impressive monument to his victory was erected in 1875 near Detmold in North-Rhine Westfalia where the battle was fought, or so they thought. However, archaeological evidence would later prove that the Battle of Teutoburgerwald was fought in an entirely different location. It wasn't until 1987 that The Late Tony Clunn MBE, a British Army officer and amateur archaeologist serving with the British Army in Germany, found the first clues. Armed with just a metal detector and a little local knowledge, his spare-time fieldwork led archaeologists to solve a 2,000-year-old mystery. There were no less than 750 potential sites for the battle when he began his search, but his book, *In Quest of the Lost Legions*, describes how old documents eventually guided him to fields where over the centuries farm workers had found a significant number of Roman coins. After months of work meticulously plotting his finds, including 160 Roman denarii, a starburst pattern began to emerge as if the coins had been dropped in a sudden and desperate hurry to flee an ambush. Archaeologists were alerted and a decade later there was sufficient evidence to proclaim beyond any shadow of doubt that Varus' last stand was near Kalkriese Hill, close to the town of Osnabruck. A museum now stands at the spot where the final assault took place.

A few words about Aethelstan are fitting at this stage because he receives but the briefest mention in the Anglo-Saxon Chronicles, despite him being a remarkably just, charitable and popular ruler, as Palgrave noted:

> When the good folks of the boroughs began to regard it as conducive to their welfare and importance that they should be able to send members to the House of Commons, Aethelstan's charter was pleaded more than once, as the foundation for their parliamentary right; and throughout the west of England there was scarcely a town in which a statue of Aethelstan was not erected. Aethelstan's charity probably contributed to his popularity. He directed that each of his royal manors should be subject to an annual charge in favour of the wretched and destitute. The steward or reeve was once in every year to redeem a slave from captivity. When criminals among the Anglo-Saxons could not pay the fines imposed upon them, they were in some cases reduced to servitude; and it was these unfortunate individuals whom Aethelstan thus intended to relieve. Furthermore, it was his pleasure that upon every two of his royal manors, the stewards should feed and clothe one poor Englishman, if he can be found.

But in the north, people were not entirely receptive to Athelstan as their overlord. Palgrave:

> They cast off their allegiance and sent for Olave, a king of the Eastmen or Danes, settled in Ireland to reign over them. Olave, however, seems to have been restored by the will and wishes of the English, as well as of the Danes, for Wulfstan,

Archbishop of York, was his most powerful supporter and continued a steady adherent of the independent party to the very last.

Aethelstan's death only two years after his famous victory at Brunanburh triggered a collapse of the English hold on York, which once again fell into Viking hands. This situation was reversed in AD 944 when king Edmund overcame the Vikings throughout Northumbria and retook York. Two years later Edmund was assassinated and the city elders chose the Viking, Eric Bloodaxe, as their king. This was despite having previously sworn allegiance to Eadred, the English king who had succeeded Edmund, and it would have severe repercussions. In AD 948 Eadred took his revenge on the Northumbrians to the extent of burning down Ripon Minster. On Eadred's homeward journey, the Danish force in York counterattacked and slaughtered the troops that he had left behind in Castleford. Fearful of the consequences, the Northumbrians abandoned their new leader and in AD 954 Eric Bloodaxe met his end in a treacherous ambush in the Pennines near the remote border of North Yorkshire with Cumbria. The Rey Cross at Stainmoor reputedly marks the site of the battle (Baring Gould). Eric was destined to be York's last Viking king.

Eadred himself died the following year, but it wasn't until the reign of Aethelred II, the boy king who was crowned king in AD 978, that invasion loomed once again. Attacks by the Danes on the shores of Britain had been conspicuous by their absence since Aethelstan's reign, but across the North Sea, a strong Scandinavian force was gathering under King Harald of Denmark or 'Bluetooth' as he was nicknamed. He had successfully united his kingdom with that of Norway and had assembled a fearsome army led by his son, Swein. Aethelred bought off the threats with Danegeld, but in the third year of his reign the Viking raids restarted. In AD 993 a Viking force entered the mouth of the Humber and according to the Chronicles 'did much evil' in Northumbria and Lindsey [Lincolnshire]. And it was the same again the following year when Swein, accompanied by Olave, King of Norway, attacked London with ninety-four ships. In the meantime, Aethelred had abandoned London and taken refuge on the Isle of

Wight, while the Viking force turned northward once again after having been paid Danegeld to the value of £16,000. It was, unfortunately, not stipulated that the Danes should leave English waters, so Swein and his fleet merely entered the Humber and ventured along the Trent as far as Gainsborough. Northumbria quickly bowed to him, as did all the folk of Lindsey, followed by the Five Boroughs (Derby, Leicester, Lincoln, Nottingham and Stamford). Soon everywhere north of Watling Street was under his control and Swein was effectively in charge of all England. But he would only live for another year before being succeeded by his son Cnut (or Canute) who became the first Danish king of all England.

Every payment made to the Danes was an open invitation to repeat the same threat at some future date and sure enough another precarious truce was purchased within a year, but this time it would cost £24,000, plus the usual supply of food. Palgrave put the payment of Danegeld into perspective when he wrote:

> Fifty thousand pounds had now been paid as Danegeld. Each pound was then equivalent in weight of silver, to somewhat more than three pounds of our nominal currency. But the intrinsic worth of the coin affords no adequate measure of its value. And the worth of fifty thousand pounds in the reign of Aethelred will be understood by knowing that this sum would have purchased about one million two hundred thousand acres of arable land together with such rights and privileges in the common lands and woods appertaining to the enclosed land.

This estimate was based on ordinary land priced at £5 of silver per hide, where one hide represents the amount of land sufficient to support a household, which equates to 120 acres [49 hectares]. It was a win-win situation for the invaders, or as Palgrave put it:

> The Danes continually retreated from the coast and the English pursued them in vain. In the end, no other consequences were produced excepting vexation to the people, waste of money, and increase of strength to the enemies. Even when

the king summoned the whole power of Wessex and of Mercia, the Danes went where so ever they would, while the undisciplined English militia, raised for the defence of the country, did more harm to the people than any external foe.

The legacy of the Danes can still be seen today in many of the place names of settlements they founded, which have endured for a millennium or more. For instance, villages and towns with names ending in 'by', meaning a place of abode, 'thorpe', meaning an offshoot or secondary hamlet, and 'holm' or 'holme', meaning an island of raised ground surrounded by marshes. We know from an Icelandic manuscript (*Egill's Saga*) dating from 1240 and covering the years AD 850–1000 that a Viking called Egill Skallagrimsson was shipwrecked 'at the mouth of the Humber' in or around AD 950 at a place that later became known as Hrafnseyrr or Ravenser, meaning Raven's beach or sand bank in Old Norse. The village of Ravenser and the town of Ravenser Odd, where 'Odd' means headland, were both engulfed by the sea many years ago.

Street names, such as Coney Street in York, where Coney means king, also show their Scandinavian origins. It is believed that Eric Bloodaxe, who had been forced to flee Norway and established himself as viceroy in York, lived at the king's palace in Coney Street. Other vestiges remain in today's division of Yorkshire into North, West and East Ridings or 'thirds'. Many of the place names recorded in the Domesday Book are of Scandinavian origin, such as Holderness, where 'hold' means a high-ranking Danelaw officer and 'ness' means a promontory. In the North and East Riding, many of the place names show a Danish origin. This, however, is not the case in the West Riding where there are considerably fewer. The Danes not only influenced the East Yorkshire dialect, they even influenced the system of land measurement. Unlike the 'hide', as found outside Danelaw, the 'oxgang' was customary in East Yorkshire and has only recently died out (Barley 1939). Their influence on art within the riding can still be seen in ancient carved stones, such as the cross inside the church of St James at Nunburnholme on the western-edge of the Yorkshire Wolds and a carved tombstone fragment at All Saints

Church in Barmston on the Holderness coast. The Nunburnholme Cross (Figs. 9a and 9b) formed part of the church fabric before it was discovered during demolition work in 1873. Predating the church itself, the cross is believed to be the work of two or possibly three sculptors from the Late Saxon to Viking and Norman periods. The carved tombstone fragment in Barmston church (Figs. 10a and 10b) is believed to be half of its original size and was created at a time when North Yorkshire was a centre of excellence for sculpture that blended a number of ancient artistic styles. There is reportedly a similar stone at St James Church in the nearby village of Lissett, although the author was unable to access the latter when he visited. Indeed, the art style known as 'Jellinge', after the stone found in Denmark, was developed in Yorkshire and owed its genesis to a mixture of Celtic, Scandinavian and Anglian styles. Four ancient crosses at St Andrews Church in Middleton near Pickering are believed to have been carved in the last quarter of the ninth century and are typical of the initial period of settlement of England when Christianity was just beginning to impact on a loosely pagan people (Wilson 1970).

Not all places settled by the Danes retained hints of their origins. In a paper delivered to members of the Hull Literary Club in 1895, J.R. Boyle wrote:

Halfdene's partition of Deira-land among the followers can only have been the beginning of the Danish colonisation. Indeed, conquest and colonisation pass necessarily through the same phases in all ages. Let the pioneer army conquer and win a new country, of richer soil and fairer climate than that of the land whence they sailed, and hosts of families of the same nation will soon flock thither. We know as well as if the chronicle or saga had told the story that in the years that followed Halfdene's conquest of Deira, fleets of Danish ships sailed ever and anon into the Humber, bringing hither families who sought not warfare, but peaceful settlement. We know more than this. We know that many of their ships found harbour in the creek around which since has grown up the port that, pre-eminently for the ports of the Baltic and the

Netherlands, has for centuries, and is still the gateway into England. On the western bank of this creek they landed, and, because of their coming, here sprang up a port – a town – which they called The Creek Town – the Vik – the name it retained till the greatest of the Plantagenet kings, the father of English law, the fosterer of English commerce, bought it and called it King's Town upon Hull.

Boyle was of course referring to Edward I, who in 1293 acquired the town from the monks at nearby Meux abbey. The story goes that Edward's hunting party chased a hare along the banks of the River Hull to the hamlet of Wyke and that the king, delighted with the lie of the land, thought that it might be the ideal spot to build a town for the defence of the realm (Craggs 1817). Indeed, the port was used by Edward for waging war against the Scots and it subsequently grew and prospered through exports of wool and imports of wine and timber. Although no archaeological evidence of the Viking settlement of Hull has been found to date, Boyle's reference is to the old name of 'Wyke' given to the site, which is derived from the Scandinavian 'vik', meaning creek.

In addition to place names bearing clues to the origins of settlements, their location also speaks volumes. The Danes tended to shy away from Anglo-Saxon villages where more unsettled land was available. This resulted in roadside settlements at which new roads sometimes branched off at right angles. The pattern, according to Boyle's theory, was that where English settlements were most numerous the Danish settlements were few and small, and where English settlements were few, Danish settlements were numerous and large. In addition, the isolation of settlements due to expanses of marshland or meres between them, reinforced differences in speech that are traceable in the East Riding even today. Although Holderness may appear to be relatively flat compared with other regions of Yorkshire, it consists of a series of low hills and gentle slopes, each of which is occupied by a village and its ancient arable lands and pastures. It wasn't until comparatively recently that the vast expanses of impassable low land between settlements were drained, making them accessible.

Their former isolation has contributed to perpetuation of a form of speech without a definite article. So, for instance, instead of saying, 'I'm going to the church, or the market,' it would be pronounced, 'I'm going t'church or t'market.' Also the system of land culture was quite different to everywhere else until enclosure – the series of acts of parliament which enclosed open fields and common land in England and Wales, creating legal property rights to land that was previously considered common.

A significant fact relating to the influence of the Danes also emerges when population returns given in the Domesday Book are analysed. Boyle observed that there are wide differences between the populations of districts colonised by the Danes and those colonised by purely English inhabitants. In Yorkshire and Lincolnshire, for instance, where the Danish influence was strongest, there were no 'servi' or slaves at the time of the Domesday Survey. In counties such as Nottinghamshire, where there was some Danish influence, only one serf in every two hundred of the population was mentioned in the returns, meaning that there were fewer servi. Boyle goes on to show how the numbers of slaves increase to almost a quarter of the total population in the counties outside Danelaw. Contrary to what we might think, this leads us to conclude that wherever the Danes dominated the population, they appear to have reduced slavery.

The next we hear from the chroniclers about matters northern is the death of Earl Siward of Northumbria in AD 1055. He was buried in St Olaf's minster, which he had ordered to be built at Galmanho, a former area of York where he is believed to have lived. The name Galmanho lives on in Galmanhoe lane at the top of Marygate. It was around this time that the succession to the English throne began to dominate politics. Edward the Confessor was perceived as a weak king throughout his long reign and was without an heir. To make matters worse, there were several potential claimants to the throne. This would have serious consequences in the years ahead and we now fast-forward a decade to two import events. The first was the banishing of Earl Tostig of Northumbria, the brother of Earl Harold (Godwinson or Godwine's son), who was overthrown in a rebellion and would later join forces with Harald Hardrada in battle against his brother at

Stamford Bridge near York. His departure was acrimonious to say the least because all of the thanes in Yorkshire and Northumberland had outlawed earl Tostig and killed as many of his men that they could find, regardless of their origin. In York they also confiscated all of Tostig's arms, possessions and money before choosing a new earl. The other important event was the death of King Edward who was taken ill in Westminster on Christmas Eve and died on Twelfth night (5 January) AD 1066. The last entry in the Chronicle for that year was significant and had an ominous ring to it. It merely stated that earl Harold was appointed king and that he had little peace during the time he ruled the kingdom. Indeed, Harold was crowned on the day Edward was buried, but he would soon be the last of the Saxon kings due to another threat that was emerging from across the North Sea.

Following his banishment from Northumbria, Harold's brother, Tostig, had returned from refuge in Flanders and sailed to the Isle of Wight with as many troops as he could carry. He would soon head north and enter the Humber with sixty ships. His fleet, however, was dispersed by Earl Edwin, and Tostig would eventually sail to Scotland with just twelve small vessels. But this was of no consequence as he was met there by King Harald Hardrada of Norway and a fleet of 300 ships in which they both returned to the Humber. They would sail on to York and defeat Earl Edwin and his brother Morcar.

There had been bitter rivalry between Tostig and his brother Harold. To make matters worse, there was some opposition to Harold's succession to the crown and he was certainly not welcomed as king by the people of Northumbria. Palgrave wrote:

> Admitting that the prelates, earls, aldermen, and thanes of Wessex and East Anglia had sanctioned the accession of Harold, their decision could not have been obligatory upon the other kingdoms; and the very short interval elapsing between the death of Edward and the recognition of Harold, utterly precludes the supposition that their consent was even asked.

Palgrave's take on the fateful happenings of AD 1066 is that the Norwegians' presence in Britain was at the instigation of Tostig, who had previously but unsuccessfully applied to the king of Denmark for support. The large Norwegian fleet, which was allegedly carrying half of the population of Norway, had called in at the Shetland and Orkney isles before arriving off the shore of Cleveland and Scarborough, where it put in and accepted the submission of the inhabitants. It later returned to the Tyne where it was joined by Tostig. The combined fleets then entered the Humber and in August landed at Ricall, just to the south of York. In September they were met by all the forces that Edwin and Morcar could muster, but to no avail. After a bitter conflict at what became known as the Battle of Fulford (a village on the outskirts of York), the citizens of York opened the city gates to the victorious Viking force. The news soon reached Harold, who in full expectation of an invasion by Duke William of Normandy, was busy mustering forces to meet the threat from across the Channel. Having gathered a huge army and fleet, he rallied his forces before marching north to York, where he arrived four or five days after its surrender on 25 September.

The Anglo-Saxon Chronicle deals fleetingly with the battle at Stamford Bridge, merely stating that King Harold surprised the Norwegians and met them beyond York with a great host of English and that there was a fierce battle in which Harald Hardrada was killed and that Tostig was put to flight together with the surviving Norwegians. Palgrave, however, adds some interesting dimensions from another source, presumably the writings of Henry of Huntingdon (1088–1157), the Anglo-Norman cleric and historian, or Snorri Sturlson (1179–1241), the Icelandic historian, poet and politician. Apparently Harold offered Tostig the earldom of Northumbria before the onslaught, but when Tostig asked him what incentive he was offering Hardrada, Harold retorted, 'Seven feet of ground for a grave!' No further deal being on the table, Harold force-marched his troops from London to Yorkshire, a distance of about 185 miles (298 km), in only four days. The Norwegians, who were expecting to receive further hostages and supplies from the Northumbrians at their Stamford Bridge camp, were caught unawares when Harold suddenly arrived at the head of an army. According to Palgrave, the Norwegian's formed a circle or 'fortress of shields' that was initially impenetrable, causing the English to retreat (or feign retreat?), at which the Norwegians broke ranks in pursuit. Just when it looked as though the English had no stomach for the fight, they wheeled around in a counter-attack. Having been struck by an arrow, Hardrada was killed in the first wave of fighting and Tostig assumed command. But he would die in the second wave of fighting after refusing Harold's offer of quarter. In the third onslaught and despite many English casualties, the Norwegians were wiped out to a man. Heaps of blanched bones are reputed to have littered the battle field until long after the event.

But what is fact and what is fiction? The precise location of the battlefield is unknown, although there is an area known as Battle Flats just southeast of the town on the east bank of the River Derwent. The exact location of the Norwegian camp is also unclear. Were Norwegian troops encamped on the west or the east bank, or both? If they were on both banks, credibility is given to the story about a Viking warrior single-handedly holding up the entire English army and only succumbing when killed by a spear that was thrust through the planks in the bridge. But did a bridge even exist at that time, or was there merely a ford? It might be presumed that the Romans built a bridge over the Derwent at this spot, but no record or evidence remains and it is more likely that a ford simply existed where the river could be crossed. One feasible theory holds that the name, Stamford, is derived from a combination of the words stone and ford, and there is an outcrop of stone in the river bed that indeed may have been a crossing point in earlier times. But there was no mention of a village by the name of Stamford at the time of the Domesday Survey some twenty years later, so was there even a place called Stamford at the time of the battle? In the latter stages of the conflict, the Norwegians were allegedly reinforced by troops who had been guarding their ships. By the time they arrived from Ricall, a distance of 12 miles as the crow flies, many of the Norwegians were in a state of collapse when they engaged the English and were either overwhelmed or drowned in the waters of the Derwent. In the aftermath of the battle, the few surviving Norwegians pledged never to attack England again and were allowed to leave for Orkney. There were so few that it required just 24 of the 300 ships from the fleet to carry them away.

As the English scholar, Alcuin of York (AD 735–804), pointed out, the like of the Vikings had never been seen before in Britain. Such ferocity, such terror, such bringers of doom! And yet there was clearly another side to them that no one outside their homelands had ever seen. They were navigators and explorers who travelled widely throughout and beyond Europe, exploring Russia, and Persia, and reaching America. They were traders: Arabic and even eastern coins have been found in Scandinavia showing that they must have traded far and wide. Perhaps most surprising of all is that despite being pagans with a fearsome reputation, they would embrace Christianity and contribute to Britain's cultural development. However adventurous, fearless and independent the Vikings may have seemed when they first came to our shores, they would settle into the traditional pastoral and agrarian ways of their homelands, just like the Anglo-Saxons had done before them. More than one authority has voiced the opinion that clerics who wrote the chronicles may have adversely coloured the reputation of the heathen Vikings, who were not the only ones to burn and pillage monasteries. From portrayals in later sagas the leaders of Viking raids seemed to lack any fixed belief in anything outside themselves and their own strength. The nicknames given to the Viking leaders, suggests a certain unceremonious and informal honesty in their descriptions of one another (Binns 1963). If this assumption is correct, we must credit the monks with some accuracy in their writings during the period when Eric Bloodaxe arrived on these shores. Having butchered no less than five of his brothers, he had, after all, more than earned his nickname (Baring Gould 1913).

Fig. 1: Victoria Cave.

Fig. 2: Duggleby
Howe.

Fig. 3: Rudston
Monolith.

Figs. 4a and 4b: The Devil's Arrows.

Fig. 5a: Skipsea Brough photographed from the west.

Fig. 5b: Impression by A. Renou of the early Norman earth and timber fortress at Skipsea.

Fig. 6: York's Bar Wall at twilight photographed by Dennis Bromage.

Fig. 7: Beverley Minster from the southwest.

Fig. 8: Whitby Abbey photographed by Dennis Bromage.

Figs. 9a and 9b: The Nunburnholme Cross.

Figs. 10a and 10b: Barmston tombstone fragment.

Figs. 11a and 11b:
The Battle of the
Standard as depicted
in All Saints Church,
Helmsley.

Figs. 12a and 12b: The ruins of Fountains Abbey on a fine spring day.

Figs. 13a and 13b (*opposite above*): The deserted medieval village of Wharram Percy.

Fig. 14: A night shot of the Shambles in York taken by Dennis Bromage.

Fig. 15: Flamborough Head, the North Landing.

Fig. 16: Blackburn B2 biplane flying over Yorkshire.

Fig. 17 (*above left*): The Blackburn Buccaneer at the RAE Bedford after its maiden flight in 1958.

Fig. 18 (*above right*): A First World War recruitment poster by Lucy E. Kemp-Welch.

Chapter 5

The Normans

Harold had only a brief moment of respite to celebrate his victory at Stamford Bridge. The following day news reached him of a new threat in the south and he would shortly face a superior invading army that was better equipped, better trained and better prepared, especially in the sense of being well rested. Encouraged by the death of Henry I of France, which reduced the chances of an invasion of Normandy by the French, Duke William of Normandy had turned his focus on England, where he believed he was the legitimate heir to the throne. On 28 September 1066, he stepped ashore on the south coast of England and his timing could not have been better. Having force-marched his troops north to fight Tostig and Hardrada, Harold now had to do the same in reverse to intercept the invading Norman army, except this time he didn't have anything like the same number of men. Many of his best troops had fallen during the battle and the few recruits that joined him on his homeward march did so south of the Humber; not a single man joined him from north (Palgrave 1876). As every history student knows, less than three weeks after the battle at Stamford Bridge, the Normans engaged and defeated the English army at Hastings, during which Harold was killed. Long lamented as the last Anglo-Saxon ruler of England, Harold has often been viewed with unusual partiality, but Palgrave questioned the justification for such feelings:

> He had no clear title to the crown in any way whatever. Harold was certainly not the heir: Edward's bequest in his favour was very dubious; and he failed to obtain that degree of universal consent to his accession, which upon the ordinary principles of political expediency, can alone legalise a change

of dynasty. The Anglo-Saxon power had been fast verging to decay. As against their common sovereign, the earls were rising into petty kings. North of the Humber, scarcely a shadow of regular government existed; and even if the Normans had never trod the soil of England, it would have been scarcely possible for the son of Godwin to have maintained himself in supreme authority.

There is still some uncertainty and speculation as to whether Harold actually fell at the Battle of Hastings, or was secreted away from the field. A chronicler of Malmesbury wrote that his corpse was handed over by William to Harold's mother for burial in the abbey of the Holy Cross, but the annals of Waltham Abbey record that two of their brethren who observed the battle from a distance approached William afterwards and asked for his permission to look for Harold's corpse. This they did but without success until they enlisted the help of Harold's first wife, who identified a mutilated and decomposing corpse that was taken back to Waltham Abbey for burial. Years later, a one-eyed and deeply scarred recluse confessed on his death-bed to attendant monks from St John's Abbey, Chester, that he was in fact Harold Godwinson. The story goes that he was carried from the field where he eventually recovered from his injuries. Naturally, the monks of Waltham Abbey disregarded this claim when it came to light and proceeded to exhume Harold's remains to ascertain whether or not they bore the same signs of injury that Harold was know to have sustained (an arrow that entered his skull through an eye socket). The story that he may have survived seems plausible enough, but Palgrave aptly summed up the theory with these words:

> We cannot find any reason for supposing that the belief in Harold's escape was connected with any political artifice or feeling. No hopes were fixed upon the usurping son of Godwin. No recollection dwelt upon his name as the hero who would sally forth from his seclusion as the restorer of Anglo-Saxon power. That power had wholly fallen, and if the humbled Englishman, as he paced the aisles of Waltham,

looked around, and having assured himself that no Norman was near, whispered to his son that the tomb which they saw before them was raised only in mockery, and that Harold still breathed the vital air – he yet knew too well that the spot where Harold's standard had been cast down was the grave of the pride and glory of England.

The Norman conquest of England had begun well for William, but it did not bode well for Northumbria. On Whit-Sunday, 1067, the day William's consort, the lady Mathilda, was crowned queen at Westminster, William was informed of an insurrection in the north. His response was to proceed to Nottingham, where he built an earth and timber castle before moving on to York where he built two more. These early castles were a key tool in William's conquest plans and he and his barons would build them throughout the land. Yorkshire has some fine examples and depending on their strategic importance many would later be developed in stone, such as the one on the east bank of the River Ouse in York where Cliffords Tower now stands. Just a stone's throw away on the opposite bank of the river and close to the city wall is another earthwork, which is all that remains of the second castle that William built in York. Easily overlooked, it was never developed in stone and became enclosed in the city's new stone walls when they were developed in the thirteenth century. Originally it stood well outside the city walls.

Having left Earl Robert in charge of Northumbria, William was incensed the following year when both the earl and 700–900 of his men were put to the sword at Durham in a revolt. Swift reprisals would soon follow when William duly arrived at York with a superior force. A chronicler summed up the inevitable taking of revenge, saying that those who could not flee, which was many hundreds of men, were killed and the borough ravaged. Disgrace and outrage was brought to St Peter's Minster. Notwithstanding William's fearful reputation and the obvious strength of his forces, it was no deterrent to the Vikings who persisted with their raids. The Danes had not forgotten Canute's eighteen-year reign as King of England and had it not been for the Norman conquest, the land might well have remained under

Scandinavian influence. In 1069, their willingness to side with the English resistance against the new enemy from Normandy led to three of king Swein's son's sailing up the Humber with 240 ships to fight alongside Edgar the Atheling, the young pretender to the English throne. He was Aethelred's great-grandson and only in his early teens when King Edward died. They were met amid great rejoicing by the Northumbrians, who were led by Waltheof, the last of the Anglo-Saxon earls. The encounter that followed was a rout in which the combined Viking and English forces took York, killing many Normans in the process. William was not amused. Once again he marched north with all the troops he could muster and remained in York for the winter while the Viking force, which had heard of William's approach, wisely abandoned the town and escaped across the Humber to the isle of Axholme. Meanwhile, William was forced to divert his attention to uprisings that were occurring in Mercia and other parts of the country. After a successful campaign, he heard that the Danes and English were again threatening York. Unable to cross the River Aire due to the bridge at Pontefract having been destroyed, William was delayed in his progress north and he failed to reach York before it was retaken by the enemy. When he did arrive, he uncharacteristically but astutely bought off the Danes, who promptly abandoned the English cause. As part of the pay-off agreement, the Danes were allowed to spend the winter near the Humber. But in a punitive response to the rebellious English, William then laid waste the entire shire in what became known as the Harrying of the North. The widespread destruction had started as a tactical ploy to isolate York before its retaking, but it ended as a severe lesson in which villagers as far away as Teesdale in the north and Beverley to the south east were forced to flee for their lives while their homes burned.

In 1075, 200 Viking ships led by Cnut, the son of King Swein once again entered the Humber and sailed to York, burning and plundering the minster before they left. But they would subsequently perish, although precisely when and how is not mentioned by the chronicler. One assumes this was at William's hand. In the meantime, resistance to William had much declined and it was only in 1085 that we again hear of a Danish force under Cnut (now the new king of

Denmark), allied to Earl Robert of Flanders, planning but not actually launching an invasion in William's absence. One chronicler suggested that a likely reason for the Danes' reluctance was the fact that William had caught wind of what was afoot and hurried to England with the largest force of cavalry and infantry from France and Brittany that he could muster. On arrival in England some wondered how the troops could all be fed. This problem never actually arose because when the invading force decided not to show up, William simply let his troops disperse. But first he laid waste the land close to the sea so that the invaders would only find scorched earth if and when they arrived.

By 1086, William had rewarded those Norman nobles who had fought alongside him by giving them land originally held by Anglo-Saxon landowners, barely 3 per cent of whom remained in possession of their land. He chose this particular moment in time – twenty years after the invasion – to commission the Domesday Survey, so called because it represented the final word in any land dispute. Why he did so is not entirely clear, but it was a remarkable feat, especially in terms of the speed with which it was put together. The returns made to the Domesday commissioners basically amounted to an assessment of the land, the labour force or population, miscellaneous sources of profit – meadow, woodland, mills, churches, fisheries – and the cash value at the time of the survey (Brooks 1966). A sad fact relating to Domesday is how it reflects the devastation that was suffered in Yorkshire at the hands of the Conqueror during the Harrying of the North in the winter of 1069–70. 'We trace its effects on every page, almost in every line of the Yorkshire Survey,' commented Boyle. 'The entry, "it is waste," is endlessly repeated. "In the time of King Edward, it was worth twenty shillings, forty shillings, a hundred shillings, now it is worth nothing," occurs again and again.' And this was the case throughout the shire. Brooks observed:

This meets us all over Yorkshire, along the coast, where places like Falsgrave and Bridlington are waste, in Cleveland, in the Vales of York and Pickering, in the West Riding dales and the Pennines. Craven is in much the same condition. Of Earl Alan's great estate, the later honour of Richmond, it is recorded that within his castlery, presumably Swaledale and Wesleydale down to the Vales of York, he had 199 manors of which 108 were waste.

It would be many decades before the land and population would recover from the blow and William would regret and confess his pitiless brutality towards innocent and defenceless victims towards the end of his life, which was much nearer than he could possibly have imagined. At the end of 1086, he was back in Normandy and in July the following year he led his troops on an expedition into France. On his return he fell ill and never recovered. He was buried in Normandy at the abbey he had founded in Caen.

Prior to 1066, Yorkshire had been a prosperous, indeed wealthy county. In 1086, it was poverty stricken from the pounding it had received and not just at the hands of the Normans. Brooks wrote:

> There is no doubt that the activities of William, the Scots and the Vikings had left northern England in a sorry state. Simeon of Durham is particularly eloquent on the iniquities of the Scots, who carried off into slavery all the able-bodied men and women they could lay their hands on, and remorselessly slew children in arms and old people.

The recovery, partially aided by the arrival of monks who began founding religious communities and abbeys in England around this time, would eventually arrive, but Brooks takes a different view about Yorkshire:

> It did not, as is often suggested, have to wait for the Cistercians to reclaim the waste. No doubt they did their share, but by the second quarter of the twelfth century the process of reclamation was well on the way. Towns like Scarborough, Whitby, Bridlington are all in good condition by the reign of Henry I (1100–1135), and the Pipe Rolls show that royal manors like Scalby, Driffield, and Pocklington are prosperous and valuable by the mid–century.

Nonetheless, the year 1086 was a watershed in the history of the county. From this point onwards rehabilitation would begin and by 1138 the Norman lords and their tenants would be in a position to put a sizable army into the field and score a decisive victory over the Scots at Northallerton. Yorkshire was effectively the border of England with Scotland at this time and the new landowners became not just an occupying force, but also a protective one. Unlike King Edward, who apart from York only held a handful of manors in Yorkshire (Aldborough, Knaresborough and Wakefield), William had kept for himself most of the Yorkshire lands that he had confiscated from earls Morcar and Tostig and added many more. 'The new Norman rulers were destined to be more interested in Yorkshire than the kings of Wessex had ever been,' observed Brooks.

Chapter 6

The Anarchy

For seventy years after the Norman Conquest, England enjoyed strong government and the benefits of royal justice, but during the 'nineteen long winters' of Stephen's reign, England knew, once again, what it was like to be governed by a weak king (Delderfield 1966). A problem arose when William the Conqueror's fourth son, Henry I, who had lost his two sons at sea in 1120, nominated his daughter, Matilda, as successor to the throne. When Henry died in 1135, the ruling council viewed a woman as unfit to rule and chose Henry's nephew and grandson of William the Conqueror, Stephen of Blois, as his successor. Civil war ensued with the nobility taking either Stephen's or Matilda's side. As Matilda was the niece of King David of Scotland, he naturally took her side and used the opportunity to try and expand his kingdom beyond Northumberland. The aggression of the Scots mounted during the reign of Stephen (1135–1154) and in 1136 they invaded northern England. A truce was agreed in exchange for the towns of Carlisle and Doncaster, but two years later everything would come to a head on Cowton Moor near Northallerton. Heading south again with a vast army, David found what was effectively an army of Yorkshiremen blocking his way. The men were spiritually led by Thurstan, the Archbishop of York, who had negotiated the truce with the Scots two years earlier. But the real leaders of the fighting force were William, Count of Aumale, Walter l'Espec, High Sheriff of Yorkshire and the barons de Gant, de Lacy, de Brus, Balliol, de Mowbray, Percy, Fossard and Stuteville. They had marched their men from York to meet the enemy under the saintly banners of Peter of York, John of Beverley, and Wilfrid of Ripon.

The Scots came into view at daybreak on the morning of 22 August 1138 and threw themselves at the foe. Despite the ferocity of their attack, the lightly-armed Scots would withdraw in disarray after only a few hours of fighting. It has been estimated that David's army comprised roughly 16,000 men. But unlike the smaller English force of about 10,000 well-trained men, many of whom wore armour, David's warriors had no protection other than their shields. Despite the ferocity of their attack, the lightly-armed Scots would sustain 10,000 casualties and withdraw in disarray. Another factor that may have worked in favour of the English is the outrageous behaviour of the Picts in David's army. One contemporary chronicler, Richard of Hexham, described them as, 'An execrable army, more atrocious than the pagans, neither fearing God nor regarding man, spread desolation over the whole province and slaughtered everywhere people of either sex, of every age and rank, destroying, pillaging and burning towns, churches and houses.' It has been suggested that this may have increased the resolve and fighting spirit of the English. Nonetheless, the remnants of the Scottish army were able to escape the battlefield and regroup in Carlisle. Although David had lost the battle, he was still able to consolidate his hold on Cumberland and Northumberland. But the English victory at the long commemorated Battle of the Standard (Figs. 11a and 11b) would be reason enough for Stephen to reward his cousin, William of Aumale, with the title of Earl of Yorkshire. And William's name would crop up regularly in the shire.

Having remained faithful to Stephen in the war with Matilda when others had wavered or changed sides, William's standing, military power and influence in the city of York grew to the point that he acted as a northern viceroy to Stephen during the 1140s. He would even be given the rare privilege of issuing coins from the earl's borough of Hedon in Holderness. In *The Lords of Holderness 1086–1260*, English wrote, 'In Stephen's reign William had immense power in the north. To him Stephen entrusted York, and he was described by a contemporary as "more truly the king, beyond the Humber" and "practically lord of all Yorkshire".' In tumultuous times, the barons were continuously on the look out for opportunities to increase their lands and strengthen their hold over them. And so it was with William, who built Scarborough castle (later to become the royal castle of Henry II) at a time when the Aumale lands were in Holderness to the south rather than in North Yorkshire. 'William's behaviour during the anarchy was typical of many of his contemporaries. He was, at least, consistent in his support of Stephen; but he took full advantage of the weak government to extend his territories and disregard civil and ecclesiastical law,' wrote English. The list of his documented acquisitions, or nearer to the truth seizures, were the castles at Pickering and Castleton and perhaps some of the Bigod (earls of Norfolk) lands, and the bishop of Durham's manor at Howden. His motive for targeting the latter may well have been that his grandfather had once held the manor.

Another liberty taken by William was the destruction of some North Riding villages to make a chase. According to English,

> These acts are symptoms of the weakening of royal control in the north. When a weak king ruled England and central government was feeble, as in Stephen's reign, the troubled time at the end of John's reign and in Henry III's minority, the counts extended their power, whether deliberately seeking a greater share of government or merely filling a vacuum. In this way, William le Gros became immensely powerful in the 1140s.

And the counts of Aumale would not shrink from exercising their power, even if it meant challenging the king's authority. 'In addition there runs through the counts' political behaviour a streak of northern separatism, perhaps first seen in Stephen of Aumale's attempt to gain the English throne,' (English 1979). This is a reference to William's father, Stephen, who in 1095 was involved by his father, Count Odo, in a plot to depose the Conqueror's son, William Rufus, from the throne. But Henry II would soon put a stop to anyone's dreams of challenging royal power, as Matilda's son, Henry of Anjou had been chosen to ascend the throne following the death of Stephen's son in 1153. The two sides agreed that Stephen should remain king until his death, which occurred the following year. And Henry lost no time in restoring order. Stephen had made little headway with the destruction of illegal castles and Henry repeated instructions for this work. He commanded return to the crown of all castles, towns and lands which had been seized or granted away during his predecessor's reign. In addition, he abolished all the earldoms given by Stephen to his partisans and took back the royal demesne which had gone with them (Barber 1964). We learn from the contemporary writings of Bridlington-born William of Newburgh (1136–1198) that early in 1155 Henry II came to York, and 'received back Yorkshire from the count of Aumale'. This also meant relinquishing his title, the Earl of York, but Henry wasn't finished. He would also confiscate William's castles at Scarborough, Pickering and Castleton with very meagre compensation, namely, just the manor at Driffield in East Yorkshire. I'Anson gave an insight into how the new king went about 'receiving back Yorkshire':

> Early in 1155, Henry II advanced to York with a large army and realising that resistance would be useless, William le Gros [so called due to his enormous size] surrendered his castle at Scarborough at the king's command. Doubtless Henry's first intention was to destroy the fortress, as he had destroyed so many of the castles run up in the time of Stephen, but apparently struck by the superlative excellence of the site, he decided to complete the structure, and between 1158 and 1174 erected the still partially existing keep.

Shortly after this humiliation, William seems to have retired from national prominence and spent the latter part of his life in Normandy.

This unfortunate period in our history was well recorded by monks, who painted a grim picture of the ravages endured by people living with the realities of a cruel and ruthless world.

> For every powerful man built castles ... and they filled the country full of castles. When the castles were built they filled them with devils and wicked men. Then, both night and day, they took those people that they thought had any goods, men and women, and put them in prison and tortured them with indescribable tortures to extort gold and silver; for no martyrs were ever tortured as they were. They were hung by

the thumbs or by the head, and corselets [weighted garments] were hung on their feet. Knotted ropes were put around heir heads and twisted until they penetrated their brains. They put them in prisons where there were adders and snakes and toads, and killed them like that. Some they put in a torture chamber, a chest that was short, narrow and shallow, and they put sharp stones in it and pressed the man in it so that he had all his limbs broken. In many castles there was a noose-and-trap consisting of chains of such a kind that two or three men had enough to do to carry one. It was so made that it was fastened to a beam and a sharp iron put around the man's throat and neck so that he could not in any direction either sit or lie or sleep, but had to carry all that iron. Many thousands they killed by starvation…. When the wretched people had no more to give, they robbed and burnt all the villages, so that you could go a whole day's journey and never find anyone occupying a village, nor land tilled. Then corn was dear, and meat and butter and cheese, because there was none in the country. Wretched people died of starvation; some lived by begging for alms, who had once been rich men; some fled the country. (Anglo-Saxon Chronicle)

When Henry II came to the English throne, disorder and poverty prevailed throughout the kingdom. The barons had oppressed the countryside, ravaging the crops, sacking villages, in order to maintain their private armies. As a result, almost a quarter of the country was in no fit state to pay the taxes due in the first year of his reign. The conquest of England in 1066 had caused far less damage than these internecine wars (Barber 1964). In every shire a part of the inhabitants wasted away and died in large numbers from famine, while others went with their wives and children into a grim self-inflicted exile. Villages widely famed could be seen standing empty, because the people of the countryside, men and women, young and old, had left them; fields whitened with harvest as the year drew on into autumn but those who should have cultivated them had fallen prey to famine and its companion, pestilence (William of Newburgh).

As a result of their disloyalty to Henry, the ringleaders of a rebellion in 1173–74, including Roger de Mowbray and Hugh Bigod, would be forced to relinquish their castles, which were subsequently dismantled. In Yorkshire, these included those at Thirsk and Kirkby Malzeard. An earldom that had been given to the Scottish king, William the Lion, in Stephen's reign and later claimed back by Henry II was that of Northumbria. When Henry was distracted by the aforementioned revolt, in which his sons were implicated, William took the opportunity of invading twice. The first time he advanced as far as Newcastle but was repulsed. The second time he returned with a larger army but was captured at Alnwick after being surprised in a dawn raid. He was eventually imprisoned by Henry at Falaise Castle in Normandy where, in December 1174, an agreement was signed between William and Henry in which Scotland would thereafter be subordinate to the English crown. In August the next year the two kings met in York to implement the terms of the treaty of Falaise and a procession of Scottish notables took place at York minster during which they formally professed obedience and allegiance. Among them were William and his brother David, all of the Scottish bishops and abbots, and many Scottish barons. The northern border would largely enjoy complete peace for the remainder of Henry's reign and there would be no serious altercation between the Scots and English for more than a century (Barber 1964).

Chapter 7

Land for Souls

Although the barony would have been aware when their actions were un-christianlike, they were not without a means to 'wipe the slate clean' as it were. For instance, Henry II famously did public penance for his part in the murder of Thomas Becket. He also promised to lead a crusade to the Holy Land, a promise that he never fulfilled. Instead he founded three monasteries at which the monks were expected to pray for his soul. Unlike any of his predecessors, Henry was associated with several Cistercian foundations established by his mother, the Empress Matilda, and he continued contributing to them, even more so after Becket's murder.

In common with many of the powerful families of the period, William le Gros was a great benefactor of religious houses, including Bridlington Priory, which he recompensed for damage incurred during the civil war. He also made donations to the Augustinian canons, whose mark of appreciation is visible even today in the ruined gateway at Kirkham Priory on the banks of the River Derwent between Malton and Stamford Bridge. Established around 1122, it is unquestionably the most impressive monastic ruin in the East Riding.

William also gifted land for a leper hospital at Newton near Hedon and for the Cistercian house of Meaux near Beverley, which was the first monastery in Holderness. The story goes that shortly after acquiring the land at Meaux in order to create a deer park, William was approached by a Cistercian monk from Fountains Abbey, who suggested that if he were to donate the land for founding a new abbey, he would be absolved from a vow he had taken to go to Jerusalem. Despite having already begun work on enclosing the deer park, the monk's idea struck a chord with William and the abbey was duly built. From that moment onwards the Cistercian order would dominate Holderness, as it dominated the whole of rural Yorkshire (English 1979). Owning vast tracts of land, Yorkshire monasteries were among the most prominent and powerful in the country. Their distinctive ruins decorate the landscape throughout the shire. Some, such as in Whitby and possibly St Mary's Abbey in York, lie on the site of earlier Anglo-Saxon monasteries that were founded within the ancient Kingdom of Northumbria, as indeed do Ripon Cathedral and Beverley Minster.

The age of the founding of monasteries began in 1120 and lasted for a century or more. 'The anxiety of the feudal noble for the salvation of his soul and for worldly renown,' as Barley put it, meant that the county became covered with monasteries of varying size and wealth. And the Cistercian order would prove to be the most spectacularly successful of them all. The Cistercian phenomenon began in 1098 with the founding of a small monastery at Citeaux in Burgundy. In 1109, the Englishman, Stephen Harding, became the abbot and it was under his leadership that the order enjoyed its most rapid period of growth. Within just a few decades people had flocked to join the order. By the mid-twelfth century there were well over 500 Cistercian abbeys in western Europe. With the Norman elite now firmly in control of England, monasteries were one of the few places where the English could still make their mark. English priors and abbots were effectively the heads of large corporations and thus able to keep English culture alive.

One outstanding monastic leader was Abbot Ailred of Rievaulx in picturesque Ryedale, North Yorkshire. Founded in 1131, the abbey was home to well over 600 monks in its heyday, but many of these were lay brothers. In 1134 Ailred was passing through Ryedale on his return to the Scottish court when he stopped at the abbey and liked what he saw. When the time time came to leave he mounted his horse, but didn't travel very far before glancing back at the abbey and having a sudden change of heart. He decided to stay on as a novice at the abbey and a decade later he would become the abbot of Rievaulx. Within another decade he would be an adviser at the court of Henry II. As the abbot of a great monastery, Ailred was sought after as an adjudicator in ecclesiastical disputes all over the kingdom and he gave Rievaulx an important place in the intellectual life of England (Billings 1991). Ailred died in 1167 and the infirmary where he lay during his last year at the abbey is still identifiable among the extensive abbey ruins.

Nestled in an idyllic location on the banks of the River Skell near Ripon are the ruins of the largest and best-preserved Cistercian monastery in England, Fountains Abbey (Figs. 12a and 12b). Founded in 1132 by a group of dissident Benedictine monks from St Mary's Abbey in York, it was destined to become the richest Cistercian monastery in medieval England. The Cistercians excelled at sheep farming and were the chief traders in wool with the markets of Flanders. In 1193–4, for instance, their annual wool crop would help to obtain the release of Richard I from captivity in Germany where he was being held to ransom at Trifels Castle by Henry VI, the Holy Roman Emperor. The amount being demanded for Richard's release was the unheard of sum of 100,000 marks. The chronicler, Ralph of Diceto, wrote:

> As for how the money was raised, we shall now demonstrate the devotion which the king's faithful men showed, beginning with the Church; the greater churches came up with treasures hoarded from the distant past, and the parishes with their silver chalices. It was decided that the archbishops, bishops, abbots, priors, earls and barons should contribute a quarter of their annual income; the Cistercian monks and Premonstratensian canons their whole year's wool crop, and clerics living on tithes one-tenth of their income.

In addition to boosting the coffers of the exchequer, Yorkshire monasteries also played an important role in land reclamation and utilisation. They had abundant labour with which to drain, clear and plough formerly waste or marshland areas, and they kept livestock that produced a valuable income. At Meaux, for instance, the monks tended a huge flock of sheep (12,000 in the year 1280) on land in Holderness described as the richest grazing land in the north of England. In the same year, monasteries in Bridlington, Ellerton, Kirkham, Malton, Meaux, Selby, Swine, Watton, St Mary's York, all sold wool to Flemish and Italian merchants for export. But the bulk of monastic land was devoted to arable farming and the areas of land differed greatly. At Meaux, there were above 1,000 acres, but at Sutton near Hull there were just 95 acres at a time when the average peasant freehold was perhaps 30 acres. Monasteries would also let their land to tenants, which would sometimes lead to rent issues and even revolts among tenants, as happened at Beeford in Holderness in 1356. Apart from agricultural land, another valuable source of income for monasteries was derived from what were termed 'spiritualities' or tithes and churches. Bridlington owned sixteen churches at the time of the Dissolution, while St Mary's of York owned seven of the city's churches. This was in addition to thirty-three churches in other parts of Yorkshire and others outside the county (Barley 1939).

In 1118, during the reign of Henry I, a dispute arose within the church whereby Archbishop Thurstan of York refused to submit to an oath of obedience to the Archbishop of Canterbury. A long and bitter battle ensued, which worsened during the reign of Henry II when the king and the incumbent Archbishop of Canterbury, Thomas Becket, were in conflict over judicial responsibility. The dispute arose when Henry tried to limit the powers of the church courts, which he considered were undermining his authority. During the six-year conflict, Henry understandably tended to favour the archbishop of York, who had crowned him king in 1170. Matters came to a head in 1176 when a physical confrontation between the two archbishops took place during the visit of a papal legate. A chronicler of the day recorded the event thus. When the clergy of all England were assembled at London on 14 March, the archbishop of York decided to take up the issue of seniority with the Archbishop of Canterbury, claiming that Pope Gregory the Great had spoken the words, 'Let there be between the bishops of London and York distinction of honour according to seniority of ordination,' and that because he had been ordained first he should sit on the cardinal's right hand. The Archbishop of Canterbury on the other hand said that his church was of such dignity and seniority that in line with the statutes of the fathers, royal charters and papal privileges it had always rightly claimed for itself the primacy of all England. The following Thursday the cardinal set up his chair in St Catherine's chapel at Westminster and when the Archbishop of Canterbury arrived, he had hardly sat down on the cardinal's right hand when fighting broke out. The cardinal left amid the clamour, but not before the Archbishop of York, who was among those assaulted, was heard to blame his injuries and torn clothing on the Bishop of Ely, who was assisting the Bishop of Canterbury. The matter of precedence between Canterbury and York was initially settled by Pope Alexander III who stood by Pope Gregory's original ruling and found in favour of York. In the fourteenth century, however, the precedence was reversed in favour of Canterbury.

Chapter 8

Darkest Hour

S enior clerics resorting to violence against each other was one thing, but the violence that took place on the night of 16 March 1190 would go down as one of the darkest episodes in England's history and it took place in York during the reign of Richard I. Triggered by Richard's preparations for the Third Crusade, an anti-Semitic frenzy resulted in the death of 150 Jews, which came in the wake of the king's coronation at Westminster on 3 September the previous year. After the coronation banquet, uninvited leaders of the Jewish community turned up to pay their respects against the express order of the king. 'The courtiers laid hands on the Jews and stripped them and flogged them and having inflicted blows, threw them out of the king's court,' commented one chronicler. But it would get worse.

> Some they killed, others they let go half dead. One of those Jews was so badly injured with slashes and wounds that he despaired of his life; and so terrified was he by the fear of death that he accepted baptism from William, prior of the Church of St Mary at York, and was baptised [with the name of] William. And in this way he avoided the danger of death at the hands of his persecutors. However, the people of the city of London, hearing that the courtiers had raged thus against the Jews, turned on the Jews of the city and robbed them and killed many of both sexes; they set light to their houses and razed them to ashes and embers. Yet a few of the Jews escaped that massacre, shutting themselves up in the Tower of London or hiding in the houses of their friends.

Swift justice would follow, but not on account of what had happened to the Jews:

> On the following day, the king having heard of this event, had some of those criminals arrested and brought before him. By the judgement of the court three of them were hanged on the gibbet: one because he had stolen something from a certain Christian, the other two because they had started a fire in the city, on account of which the houses of Christians had been burnt.

And the anti-Jewish violence didn't stop there. Early the following year a chronicler recorded, 'Throughout England many of those preparing to join the the crusade to Jerusalem decided they would rise up against the Jews before they attacked the Saracens.' There was further slaughter in Norwich, Stamford and at Bury St Edmunds, where reportedly fifty-seven Jews were killed. But the most shocking report of all came from York where about fifty Jews were killed, 'many of them inflicting wounds on each other. For they preferred to meet death at the hands of their own people rather than to meet death at the hands of the uncircumcised.' In reality, some 150 Jews were either massacred, committed mass suicide, or were burned alive within the wooden keep of York Castle or Clifford's Tower, as it is known today.

The story goes that rumours about the king having ordered Jews to be attacked spread to York where the leader of the Jewish community led his people into the royal castle for safety. A large mob surrounded the castle and when the constable tried to return (he had left the castle to consult the sheriff about what to do next) the Jews refused to open the door causing a siege situation. Eventually an act of collective suicide was decided upon and the castle was set on fire from within to prevent the mutilation of any Jewish corpses. Some died in the flames but the majority took their own lives. Showing a willingness to convert to Christianity, the few who surrendered were simply killed by the mob. The chronicler wrote that no wise men rejoiced at the dire and dreadful slaughter of the Jews. For his part,

Richard took steps to avoid a further act of outrageous mob-violence, but within the decade he himself would be dead and his successor, Richard's brother, John, was not about to do the Jews any favours. Many left England to escape the heavy fines he imposed, but in 1290, during Edward I's reign, all Jews would become persona non grata in England for the remainder of the Middle Ages and indeed beyond (The Plantagenet Chronicles).

King John's seventeen-year reign (1199–1216) would be memorable for many reasons, not in the least for the loss of all the vast Plantagenet dominions in France with the solitary exception of Gascony. John began his reign in the manner he intended to continue, namely, by asking for money. 'Not without some administrative ability, especially as regards the collection of money, he was cruel and avaricious,' wrote one observer, while the chronicler, Ralph, abbot of Coggeshall, recorded:

> King John, coming to the province of York, demanded money from certain Cistercian abbots who met him there, and from the other abbots of the order. He wished to oppress the order with the obligation of the tax (three shillings on each carucate of land), since until now it had been held free of payments of this kind. The abbots simply replied that they never paid any money without the common consent of the general chapter. The king was greatly irritated by their response. In anger and in fury he ordered his sheriffs that they should injure the men of that order by whatever means they could.

In 1204 John lost Normandy to the King of France and a year later only a small fragment of the vast Angevin empire would remain. In 1207 he quarrelled with the church to the point that it led to his excommunication and his abject failure at governing the country was only matched by his ability to irritate his people through unjust taxes. The most unpopular of these was the income tax of one thirteenth, or one shilling on every mark (roughly thirteen shillings), that was levied in the same year. It became a model for taxes on income as opposed to land and caused some to hide their goods in monasteries.

It even forced the king's own half-brother, Geoffrey, Archbishop of York, into exile because of his stubborn opposition to it being levied on his tenants (The Plantagenet Chronicles). But John's inevitable day of reckoning was not far away and would come on the island of Runnymede in the River Thames near Windsor in 1215.

Magna Carta, the great charter that the barons forced John to sign in June that year, was originally intended to address the issues that they, the privileged few, were experiencing thanks to John's tyranny. It grew, however, to become the foundation of English laws and liberty, thus representing a true watershed in English history. But John's problems continued and within a few months civil war broke out. He marched against the barons in the north and took Richmond castle, which was held by Roald fitz Alan, one of the leaders of the barons' revolt. The barons and knights who met there were tired of John's abuses, which were addressed by Magna Carta. And John might have even defeated the barons in 1216 and annulled the Charter, but the struggle caught up with him and he died at Newark castle on 19 October that same year. A one-liner written by a contemporary chronicler summed up the perceptions of the day. 'He was munificent and liberal to outsiders but a plunderer of his own people, trusting strangers rather than his subjects, wherefore he was eventually deserted by his own men and, in the end, little mourned.'

An example of John's tyrannical behaviour was his treatment of a simple hermit and self-styled soothsayer, who clearly hadn't the common sense to imagine the consequences of his own words. A chronicle entry for the year 1213 noted:

> There was a certain man called Peter of Wakefield. He was a simple and rustic man supporting his life on bread and water and proclaiming to the people that he could foretell the future. He preached that John's reign would not last beyond the next Ascension Day, because it had been revealed to him that King John would reign for fourteen years.

He was arrested and detained at John's pleasure until the said day had passed. Many had believed in his prophecy and John himself had not been without his doubts, but critically the French had got word of it and it was regarded as incitement to invade England. John was relieved when the day passed peacefully, but some suggested that 'Peter had disturbed the land, spread alarm and despondency among the people and encouraged the king's enemies.' This was all John needed to have Peter hanged together with his son – just in case he was complicit in Peter's prophecy.

Chapter 9

Late Middle Ages

We now move forward in time to the reign of Edward II (1307–1327) and to the Battle of Boroughbridge, which was fought between the king and a group of rebellious barons on 16 March 1322. Edward was a weak king who allowed his favourites to influence him to a degree that caused resentment among his courtiers. Before his death, Edward's father had pleaded with him not to recall the banished favourite, Piers de Gaveston, to court. But when his father died, Gaveston was often seen at court wearing the crown jewels and acting insultingly to nobles. One of these was Thomas, the earl of Lancaster, whom Gaveston derisively called the 'old hog' despite him being Edward's cousin and one of the wealthiest men in the country. Matters became worse when Gaveston was created Earl of Cornwall and Warden of the Realm. Behind his back he was called 'the witch's son' and was loathed by many at court and especially Edward's wife, Isabella, the daughter of Philip the Fair of France, who resented the attention that Edward poured on Gaveston. In 1308 the barons demanded his banishment – a fate that his enemies thought was much too lenient and that Edward dared not refuse. Stripped of his earldom, Gaveston was formally exiled and sailed to Ireland. Determined to have their say in government, a standing committee of twenty-one bishops, earls and barons was appointed to govern the realm for one year. But within a year Gaveston, or 'brother Peter', as Edward called him, was back at the king's side. In 1311 the pressure was mounting again on Edward to have his favourite removed. Kept out of harm's way in the north, Gaveston eventually fled first to France and then Flanders, but he was soon back in England. Led by Thomas of Lancaster, the barons hunted him down to Scarborough castle where after a three-weeks siege he was apprehended. Although some wished to spare him, he was taken to Blacklow Hill near Warwick where he was executed and his head taken to Edward.

Gaveston's murder only had the effect of increasing Edward's hatred of the barons. Notwithstanding what had gone before, Edward soon found a new favourite in the ambitious Hugh le Despenser, who, together with his father, received royal favours above and beyond what the barons could take. There was a call to arms and the rebel barons went on the offensive, laying siege to Tickhill castle in the West Riding before advancing to meet the royal forces. However, the rebel force became demoralised and men began to desert. Their one hope was to try and join the Scots further north, but when they reached Boroughbridge, they found themselves heavily outnumbered and the River Ure crossing already taken by Edward's forces. There was no alternative but to fight, and the rebel army was routed. Thomas, the Earl of Lancaster was taken to Pontefract castle where he was given a mock trial before being ridiculed and then beheaded, together with some thirty of his followers, including John de Mowbray and Roger de Clifford, who were executed at York. 'Savagely was the blood of Gaveston avenged, but little sympathy can be extended to the victims,' wrote one commentator. But Edward was on a downward spiral. In 1314 his large army was humiliated at Bannockburn by Robert the Bruce in a battle that secured Scottish independence. An English army had been sent northwards in August that year, but in September Edward wrote that he had found 'neither man nor beast' in the Lothians and was compelled to retreat, taking up winter quarters at Byland Abbey in the Ryedale district of North Yorkshire. Envisaging a second invasion the following year, Edward totally misread Bruce's strategy. In October he crossed the border and attacked the king's forces, driving Edward to the gates of York. The entire north was now at the mercy of the Scots who camped at Malton. So alarmed was the populace that the canons of Bridlington priory in which town Edward had stayed, removed their treasure across the Humber to a safer place (Vickers 1913). On top of this, Edward had fallen foul of Henry of Lancaster, the younger brother of Thomas, who had assumed the earldom and after Bannockburn became the most powerful man in the kingdom when he was elected president of the Royal Council.

Things came to a head in 1326 when Edward's forces faced a superior army of foreign mercenaries led by Roger Mortimer, Lord of Wigmore and Queen Isabella. Edward and Despenser fled but were later captured. Despenser was humiliated and hanged, while Edward was held in captivity until he was officially deposed and barbarically murdered in 1327, allegedly on Isabella's order.

Edward's eldest son, Edward the Black Prince, succeeded to the throne at the tender age of fourteen, ruling initially under the watchful eye of Isabella, his mother, and a regency of 14. He turned out to be the darling of the nation and during his fifty-year reign restored English pride through his success in war, notably against the French at Cressy and Poitiers. But in 1348 and 1349 the land was visited by a terrible plague that swept across Europe and devastated the country, killing half of the population (at that time estimated to have been just under 4 million). In Yorkshire, more than one half of the clergy perished. The Black Death, or simply 'The Dethe' as Chaucer referred to it in his *Prologue*, would subsequently strike three times between 1361 and 1407 with devastating effect. The loss of life was so great that labour shortages became acute. Land prices fell and the cost of labour rose to the point that labourers could virtually name their own price. Many landowners gave up letting their land for arable farming because there was no one to reap the crops. The countryside in the Middle Ages was gradually evolving towards the creation of a class of large peasant farmers and a body of wage-earning labourers. The monasteries and feudal landowners were mainly responsible for this and tenants were evicted in order that arable land might be turned to pasture and smallholdings concentrated in larger farms (Barley 1939). 'It was easier to pay one shepherd than to pay fifty labourers,' wrote Meiklejohn. Of the 2,263 villages listed in a gazetteer of deserted medieval villages in England (published in 1968), some 130 were located in the East Riding of Yorkshire, where depopulation continued to cause much unrest until as late as the seventeenth century (Beresford & Hurst 1971). Perhaps the most famous example of a deserted medieval village in England can be found at Wharram Percy (Figs. 13a and 13b) on the western-edge of the Yorkshire Wolds, just south of Wharram-le-Street. The village flourished between the twelfth and early fourteenth centuries, when it belonged to the Percy family, but gradually over two centuries it became deserted as pastureland increased and agricultural labour decreased. The final evictions took place around 1500 and the only remains visible above ground are of the ruined church. Thanks to the village's stone foundations, much of the original layout can still be seen in the surrounding fields.

It was during Edward the Black Prince's reign (1327–1377) that the name of John Wycliffe, the first English reformer and the father of English prose, came to prominence. Born in the village of Hipswell, near Catterick Camp in North Yorkshire, Wycliffe was a theologian who shared the opinion of John of Gaunt, Duke of Lancaster, that the clergy should be expelled from all secular offices on the grounds that educated laymen were capable of performing the same duties. For his part, Wycliffe strove to bring back the purity and simplicity of ancient times (Meiklejohn 1897). The English church was immensely powerful and had an income equal to about one-third of the entire kingdom. But there were laymen as well as churchmen who objected to the increasing wealth and luxury of the church. Known as 'Lollards', their dissatisfaction extended from both the doctrines of the church to the conduct of its clergy and Lollardism had a strong political element. 'The germ of socialism, which no doubt showed itself in the Lollard doctrine and in the constant demand for the abolition of the wealth of the clergy, alarmed the barons and made them strong supporters of orthodoxy,' wrote Meiklejohn. In 1377 Wycliffe and others were summoned by the Bishop of London to answer for their beliefs. The next year the Archbishop of Canterbury followed suit and a statute against heretic preachers was passed, but Lollardism continued to grow as did fears among monks and bishops. Although John of Gaunt was Wycliffe's patron and protector, his son, Henry IV, was the bitterest enemy of Wycliff's followers and became the first English king to put men to death for their religious opinions. In Richard II's reign, Parliament wouldn't even allow heretics to be imprisoned, let alone put to death, but now they were being burned on the whim of an ecclesiastic court, the first victim being claimed in 1401. The persecution lasted until Henry's death in 1413 (Meiklejohn 1897). At the end of 1384 Wycliffe suffered a stroke while saying mass and died at the age of 64. But that didn't save him from being declared a heretic and excommunicated posthumously in 1415. His writings were burned and his bodily remains were exhumed from consecrated ground, burned and the ashes thrown into the River Swift, which flows through Lutterworth in Leicestershire. In addition to being a reformer and seminary professor at Oxford, Wycliffe was an accomplished biblical translator, producing in 1382 a translation from Latin into Middle English of a volume that became known as Wycliffe's Bible.

We now turn briefly to the reign of Richard II, the last of the Angevin kings, who in 1377 succeeded his grandfather, Edward III 'The Black Prince', at the even younger age of 10. The Black Death had been followed by a time of social unrest and the Peasants' Revolt of 1381. Richard, an unjust king who was intent on ruling as an absolute monarch without any involvement of Parliament, sowed the seed for the struggle for the crown that famously became known as the Wars of the Roses, or 'Cousins' War'. Spanning the reign of seven kings of England, it had its origins in the many potential successors to the throne left behind by Edward III. The wars started in 1399 when Henry Bolingbroke, the son of John of Gaunt, the 1st Duke of Lancaster, decided to return from exile in France to reclaim the family's estates forfeited to Richard II. He landed with a handful of men at the former port of Ravenspur in Holderness at the mouth of the Humber and now reclaimed by the sea. Henry was immediately joined by the great northern families of Percy and Neville. Crucially, Richard's uncle, the Duke of York, who had been left in charge of the kingdom while Richard was away on a campaign in Ireland, allowed Henry to proceed to London unimpeded. Richard, in the meantime, returned to find that he had been deposed as king and that Henry had been been elected by Parliament as his successor and crowned Henry IV. Richard was destined to suffer a similar fate to Edward II and was held in captivity at several locations before finally being murdered in 1400 at Pontefract castle.

The first battle in the Wars of the Roses took place at St Albans in 1455 when Richard, Duke of York, and his allies, the Neville earls of Salisbury and Warwick, defeated a royal army commanded by

Edmund Beaufort, Duke of Somerset. Further battles were fought in 1459 at Blore Heath in Staffordshire, when a Yorkist force based at Middleham Castle was intercepted as it tried to link up with the main Yorkist army at Ludlow Castle in Shropshire, and again in 1460, when the king was defeated and captured at Northampton. Hoping to claim the crown, the triumphant Yorkists immediately called a Parliament. But a compromise was eventually reached whereby Henry VI would remain on the throne until his death, after which the Duke of York would succeed to the throne. Henry's wife, Queen Margaret, however, had no intention of standing by while her son, Edward, was disinherited by this arrangement and this led to further conflict at the Battle of Wakefield, which took place on the last day of 1460. The years from 1460 to 1487 formed the first truly revolutionary period in English history (Ross 1976). According to Ross:

> The Crown itself became the coveted prize of the warring factions. The results were spectacular. Within twenty-five years the crown changed hands no less than six times. The chief victims of this phase were the kings themselves and their immediate families. No less than three of the five kings involved – Henry VI, Edward V and Richard III – died violent deaths, and the families of Lancaster and York were exterminated in the direct male line.

Or, in the words of Meiklejohn, 'One-half of the nobility of England were slain in the battles.'

While Henry VI was under close house arrest, the Yorkist earls ruled in his name. Meanwhile, the queen was busy trying to assemble a new army in Hull and early in December 1460 she was joined by a host of nobles and warlike northern barons. The Yorkists responded by marching north with their own army led by Richard, Duke of York, reaching Sandal castle near Wakefield by Christmas. On 30 December Richard made a fatal mistake and left the castle with what he believed was an adequate force, but he surprisingly found himself facing Queen Margaret's superior army. It proved a disaster for the Yorkists and Richard's severed head would soon be displayed wearing a paper crown and impaled outside York's city gates. At the beginning of 1461 Lancastrian and Yorkist forces would clash again at Mortimer's Cross in the Welsh Marches when Richard's eldest son, the young Earl of March, sought revenge for his father's death against a force led by Owen Tudor. The Lancastrians were utterly defeated with terrible slaughter, but Queen Margaret's army, fresh from its victory in Wakefield, swept aside a Yorkist force led by the Earl of Warwick in a bloody encounter at the second battle of St Albans on 17 February 1461. The stage was now set for a showdown in London where both Yorkist and Lancastrian forces were headed. Margaret arrived first, but there was strong public feeling against her and her husband, Henry VI, who had in the meantime been rescued. Considering these unfavourable circumstances, Margaret withdrew and returned north leaving the popular Earl of March to enter London on 3 March 1461, where he was declared king Edward IV, thus deposing Henry. Barely a week later and at the age of just 19, Edward found himself marching north against the Lancastrians once again. This time the two enemies would engage in battle at Towton, near Tadcaster.

It was in the cold dawn of Palm Sunday morning on the 14 March 1461 that between fifty and sixty thousand men faced each other in what was destined to be the largest and bloodiest battle of the entire civil war. The previous day had seen a clash between a Lancastrian force that had attacked a Yorkist vanguard as it was attempting to cross the River Aire at Ferrybridge. The Yorkists eventually achieved a crossing slightly further upstream at Castleford and the Lancastrian force was driven north and destroyed at Dingtingdale near the village of Saxton. Early the next morning, Edward's Yorkist force advanced to face the Lancastrian army that was positioned on a ridge between Saxton and the village of Towton. The battle was fought during a blinding snowstorm that 'flew in the faces of the Lancastrian bowmen and spoilt their aim', wrote Meiklejohn. 'The Yorkists waited till their quivers were empty; marched close up to them and poured in volley after volley, and then fell upon them with sword in hand.' But the hand-to-hand fighting was still bitter and lasted six hours. At the end of it there were 33,000 corpses on the battlefield, which in

Meiklejohn's day was still referred to locally as 'Palm Sunday Field'. As was often the case, recriminations followed for those who survived the carnage but were unable to flee the field. Forty-two knights were taken prisoner and later executed. 'The day after, the axe of the executioner finished the work which the sword of the knight had begun,' wrote Meiklejohn.

> The snow was dyed crimson as it lay. The Wharfe ran red with blood. Many of the Lancastrian dead were drowned as they fled and the Yorkists cavalry cut down those who managed to escape the scene as they streamed towards Tadcaster. The dead lay for two or three days over a space of ten miles long [up to the very gates of York] and half a mile broad.

Edward's great victory hugely increased his grip on the kingdom and particularly his power in the North of England where the Lancastrian support was at its strongest. 'In spite of Lancastrian sympathies in Yorkshire, the county offered no resistance to Edward after Towton,' wrote Ross. Meiklejohn summed up the enormous significance of the battle thus. 'If we consider the numbers engaged as well as the obstinacy of the struggle, we must call this the greatest battle that had ever been fought in England since the Battle of Hastings.' Margaret and Henry, who had been waiting in York for news of the conflict, fled to Scotland and in 1464 the Lancastrians suffered further defeats at Hedgely Moor and Hexham in Northumberland. Henry was eventually recaptured and thrown into the Tower of London.

In 1464, Edward made public that he had secretly married the beautiful Elizabeth Woodville, the widow of Sir John Grey, who had been a Lancastrian supporter. Worse still, Edward showered honours upon the new favourites of his family, the Woodvilles, which raised eyebrows at court, including those of Richard Neville, the powerful Earl of Warwick. And he wasn't alone. The king's own brother, George, the Duke of Clarence, was incensed. With a view to overthrowing Edward and replacing him with Clarence, these two registered their discontent by giving their support to a peasants' uprising in Yorkshire. 'The two years from June 1469 to May 1471 form a period of political instability without parallel in English history since 1066,' wrote Ross.

> Trouble first broke out in Yorkshire late in April 1469, when a large assembly of malcontents gathered around a captain calling himself Robin of Redesdale or Robin Mend-All. They appear to have been dispersed by John Nevill, earl of Northumberland and heir to the vast Percy lands in the north-east of England. Immediately after, the earl was called upon to deal with another separate movement of discontent originating in the East Riding of Yorkshire under a leader known as Robin of Holderness, who has been identified as Robert Hilyard from Winestead [near Hull].

One source held that this second rising was in protest at the much resented claim by the Hospital of St Leonard in York to a rent of twenty-four sheaves of corn from each ploughland in the four northern counties – a demand that had caused trouble for over a century. But it was also held that the rising was intended to restore the Percy family to its rightful place. The Redesdale rebellion was generally viewed as a Neville-inspired movement in which Robin himself was probably Sir John Conyers of Hornby in the North Riding. There were hostile gatherings in Richmondshire, where John, Lord Scrope of Bolton, Sir John Conyers and other Warwick associates were involved in a so-called Wensleydale connection. But the Yorkshire rebels dispersed when Edward received their submission at York in March 1470.

In July that year there was news of further risings in the north, this time led by Lord FitzHugh of Ravensworth in the North Riding. Edward took a gamble by venturing north and leaving the south vulnerable to invasion. He arrived in August only to find that the rebels had fled to Scotland, but he lingered in Yorkshire until mid-September when the news of Warwick's landing in the south reached him. Many joined the rebel army as it marched along, which persuaded Edward to set out for London amid the mounting

discontent with his misguided government. He had barely passed
Doncaster when further news reached him of a major defection by a
former ally. Warwick's brother, John Neville, who had been made to
relinquish his earldom of Northumberland when Edward reinstated
Henry Percy to his father's forfeited title and estates, had changed
sides. His force was large and he was now looking for Edward in order
to take his revenge. Having been deserted by most of his troops and
finding himself outnumbered, Edward cut across country to King's
Lynn from where he escaped to the Continent. But on 14 March
1471, he returned with a small force of 2,000 men and landed at
Ravenspur (Spurn Point) in Holderness at the mouth of the Humber
where Henry Bolingbroke had returned from exile seventy-two years
before. Except on this occasion Edward's men were armed not with
bows and arrows, but with a new weapon that would revolutionise
warfare, namely, hand guns!

Lancastrian sympathies were strong in Yorkshire and when
Edward arrived at Hull he was refused entry. Moving further inland,
he was admitted into York only after pleading that he had returned
to recover his duchy and not to claim the throne. The city opened its
gates to him on the 18 March on the condition that he left his troops
outside the city walls and entered with just a handful of men. But
there were large bands of armed men out looking for him, one of
which was led by Martin de la See, a gentleman from Barmston in
Holderness. From York he marched to his family seat at Sandal, near
Wakefield, luckily without drawing the attention of John Neville, who
rather surprisingly had not intercepted him when he passed nearby
Pontefract castle. Despite a number of supporters joining Edward
at Wakefield, there were not as many as he had hoped for (Vickers
1913). At Doncaster he was joined by a small body of men and his
forces gradually grew as he pushed south for London, which opened
its gates to him on 11 April (Ross 1974). The rival factions met in
a test of strength at Barnet Heath near London on Easter morning,
which ended in a rout for the Yorkists and the deaths of 7,000
Lancastrians, including the turncoat, Warwick the kingmaker. The
Lancastrian resistance was finally crushed at the Battle of Tewksbury
on 4 May 1471 when Queen Margaret's army was defeated and she

herself captured, bringing to an end the Wars of the Roses. 'The great barons had almost all been killed and the great houses – especially those of the North – were rooted out, and more than the half of the nobility having perished by the sword or axe,' wrote Meiklejohn. An odd occurrence arose during the continuously shifting fortunes of the conflict when both the Lancastrian and Yorkist kings were both held captive simultaneously. Meiklejohn:

> Among the odder turns of events in this reign, Edward was himself for a short time a prisoner in Middleham Castle, Yorkshire, in the hand's of Warwick's brother, the Archbishop of York. Thus England was in the extraordinary condition of having two kings, both captive in different places, under the charge of one earl!

Whereas, on the one hand, the Wars of the Roses had been about a dynastic struggle for power between the descendants of Edward III's third son, John of Gaunt the Duke of Lancaster and his fourth son, Edmund the Duke of York, it had also been a full-scale feud between the powerful northern families – the Nevilles and Percies. 'To claim that the Neville-Percy feud was the chief single factor which turned political rivalry into civil war may be something of an exaggeration, but it certainly had implications, both immediate and long-term, of considerable importance,' wrote Ross in 1974.

> First, the bitterness and the rivalry it engendered in the north of England survived the private war of 1453–4 and powerfully influenced the struggle between York and Lancaster between 1459 and 1464. For the north of England, the true meaning of the Yorkist triumph was the victory of the Neville interest over the Percy family and their allies. For a decade the Percy interest lay in ruins, only to be revived by Edward himself at a critical point in his fortunes. Secondly, the feud soon dragged in others beside the original protagonists and helped to determine their attitudes to the struggle between York and Somerset at the centre of government.

One significant fact would result from this chapter of English history: Edward IV would prove to be the only English king ever to lose his throne and then recover it.

In contrast with the previous century, great improvements and developments in the commerce of England were now taking place and especially in Yorkshire, where the growing demand for wool was boosting the economy and the wealth of the merchant class in particular. One such merchant family, the de la Poles of Hull, rose from being mere wool merchants to being 'wealthier and more powerful than many of the members of the old nobility', wrote Meiklejohn. Having arrived in Hull as one of three orphans, William de la Pole, would eventually become prominent enough to lend money to a king of England and marry into the royal family. Acting in partnership as creditors to other merchants, the brothers William and Richard would soon be commissioned to purvey wines for the king at Hull and William became the town's first mayor. In 1337 he was able to form a consortium of English wool merchants that had a monopoly on wool exports and in 1340 he inherited the estate of another wealthy Hull merchant and landowner. By mortgaging his entire property, William played a significant part in financing Edward III during the Hundred Years' War with France. The king wrote that he was, 'bound to his beloved merchant, William de la Pole for 76,180 pounds' – an enormous sum at that time. The king rewarded William and Richard with a knighthood and a pension, and William was appointed First Gentleman of the Bedchamber. He was later made Lord of Holderness and Baron of the Exchequer. Prior to his death in 1366, he founded a hospital and monastery in Hull and lies buried in Hull Minster.

William's son, Sir Michael de la Pole, who during the reign of Richard II became the Earl of Suffolk, rose even higher than his father to become Edward III's chief financier. He also served under Edward's sons Edward, the Black Prince, and John of Gaunt, Duke of Lancaster, and later struck a close friendship with Edward's grandson and heir, Richard II. Having distinguished himself in the war with France, he was appointed Admiral of the King's Fleets and in 1383 he became Lord High Chancellor of England. Although never having been a merchant, Sir Michael was immensely rich and upon receiving his earldom built a magnificent manor house called Suffolk Palace, which stood at the corner of Lowgate and Alfred Gelder Street in Hull's old town (a site on which the General Post Office building later stood for many years). It was easily the largest secular building in the town and seventeenth-century plans show it having a tower hardly smaller than that of Holy Trinity Church – now Hull Minster (Gillett and MacMahon 1980). Clearly the palace building was important enough for Henry VIII to have the nearby church of St Mary's 'remodelled', as recorded by the antiquary Abraham de la Pryme, who spent three years in Hull from 1698:

> In the year 1538 when that sacrilegious and arbitrary prince, king Henry came to this town and resided somewhile at his pallace or manour hall here, he caused ye great body of ye sayd church of St Mary's and ye great steeple thereof to be all pulled down to ye bare ground for ye enlargement of his manour and converted all ye stone and woodwork thereof to ye walling of ye same and ye use of ye blockhouses that he then caused to be made on ye garrison side, then called Dripool side. So that there was nothing of ye sayd church left standing but ye chancel which also was not saved without great intreatys. Which chancel being very large and handsome makes a very fine church in it self, and that which is called St Mary's church to this day.

But when Richard was deposed, his ministers and favourites also fell from power and Sir Michael was driven into exile, dying in Paris in 1389. His title and estates were, however, restored to his son, Michael, in 1402, during the reign of Henry V. Despite serving his king and country with distinction at the siege of Harfleur in 1415, the second earl eventually succumbed to an illness he contracted during the campaign. Meiklejohn wrote:

> Disease and death had made great havoc in the English army and thinned it down to one-third of its original number;

the fleet was driven off the coast by bad weather, and Henry offered to give up his conquest if he were allowed to retire peacefully upon his English town of Calais. But the French, who had now assembled an army of about ten times the number of the English would listen to nothing but unconditional surrender. Henry preferred death and resolved to cut his way at all risks to Calais. With a weary, sickly, and half-starved but still courageous force, he succeeded, after making a long detour, in crossing the Somme, and found himself face to face with a French force of about eighty thousand men.

And among those men was the second earl's eldest son, Michael, who was among the fallen at the Battle of Agincourt on 24 October 1415. William de la Pole, the brother of Michael, succeeded him as the 1st Duke of Suffolk and accompanied the king on a subsequent expedition to France in 1417. He would spend no less than seventeen years away from home, his war service extending well into the reign of Henry VI and up to the siege of Orleans in 1428. 'The earl of Suffolk was in command of the troops that were besieging the town of Orleans,' wrote Meiklejohn. 'The French tried to cut off a convoy of provisions for the besiegers, but were totally defeated; and as these provisions were chiefly fish, for it was Lent, the fight is known as the Battle of the Herrings.' The town was on the brink of surrendering in April 1429, when the sudden appearance of a strange deliverer miraculously turned the tide in favour of the struggling French: enter Joan of Arc, the Maid of Orleans. 'In the midst of a terrible thunderstorm she marched through the English lines, unperceived and unopposed, and next morning showed herself on the walls of Orleans. Fort after fort fell into her hands and the English, believing they were fighting against invisible powers, raised the siege and marched away.' But this was not the only humiliation that William de la Pole would have to endure. The loss of Normandy the following year was attributed to him, as was the loss of the province of Maine. He was also accused of murdering the Duke of Gloucester and various other crimes, which resulted with his banishment by Parliament for five years. Being too lenient a sentence for the liking of his political enemies, they arranged for his abduction and decapitation following a mock trial while at sea during his journey into exile. His mutilated body was later found on the seashore near Dover and returned to Hull where it was buried at Charter House in accordance with his will. William was succeeded by his eldest son, John, who at the age of 9 was married to the 7-year-old Lady Margaret Beaufort, the daughter of Henry VI's cousin, the Earl of Somerset. However, the marriage was later annulled when John became a Yorkist and married Elizabeth Plantagenet, the sister of Edward IV and Richard III. Their marriage produced eleven children.

As the Earl of Lincoln, John succeeded Richard, Duke of Gloucester, as president of the Council of the North, an administrative body set up in 1472 by Edward IV to improve government control and economic prosperity throughout northern England. The Council initially met at Richard's castle in Sheriff Hutton to the north of York, and at Sandal Castle in Wakefield. It was re-established in 1537 by Henry VIII to manage the affairs of the northern cities in the wake of the Pilgrimage of Grace (see next chapter) when the north became identified with Roman Catholicism. After the dissolution of St Mary's Abbey in York, Henry retained the abbot's house for use by the Council, when it became known as the King's Manor. The Council, which sat for four months in the year, at Hull, York, Durham and Newcastle, was finally abolished in 1641 in the run-up to the English Civil War.

Chapter 10

Persecution, Strife and Civil War

We now move forward in time to the Tudor period and to the reign of Henry VIII, which sowed the seed for an insurrection that became known as The Pilgrimage of Grace. 'Religious opinion and the feelings of quiet people were greatly disturbed and unsettled by the Divorce Question, the severance from Rome and the suppression of the monasteries,' wrote Meiklejohn. 'The people of the North had always been conservative, regarded their monks with great favour, and saw with bitter sorrow their old thriving villages turned into bare sheep walks.' In 1535, Henry had more or less caused the needless execution of the highly respected statesman, Thomas More, and the churchman, Bishop John Fisher (1469–1535). The eldest son of a Beverley merchant, Fisher attended Beverley Grammar School and went on to study in Cambridge. He was canonised together with Thomas More in 1935.

With their martyrdom still fresh in people's minds, the counties of Yorkshire and Lincolnshire rose in rebellion, choosing a young lawyer, Robert Aske, as their leader. Aske, whose family seat was at the village of Aughton in the East Riding, not far from Selby, belonged to the gentry and was related through his mother to Lord Clifford. He wrote a letter to a governor of Beverley with instructions on how to organise a rising, which duly took place on Sunday 8 October 1536, when armed townsfolk gathered on common land known as the Westwood, signalling the start of Pilgrimage of Grace. The unrest spread throughout the riding over the next few days, during which men gathered in their thousands at Hunsley Beacon and Staxton Wold. In Malton, 10,000 met under the leadership of Sir Thomas Percy of Seamer, the Earl of Northumberland's brother. On 13 October, Robert Aske led a Howdenshire force to Market Weighton Hill where they met forces from Beverley and Hunsley Beacon before marching on York and Hull. A considerable 'army' comprising thousands (somewhere between twenty and thirty thousand has been estimated) marched on York behind the banner of St Cuthbert and entered the city unopposed on 16 October. Hull was taken on 20 October following the arrival of reinforcements from York. The rebels then marched on Pontefract, where Lord Darcy had little option but to surrender the castle and take the pilgrim's oath. He would later explain to Henry that his defensive force was insufficient to keep out the rebels, but privately Henry suspected Darcy's complicity in the insurrection, as well as that of the Archbishop of York who was also in Pontefract at that time and took the pilgrim's oath before being released.

The entire countryside was soon in the hands of the pilgrim army, which now numbered between thirty and forty thousand strong. Military posts were set up from Hull to Newcastle and the army next marched on Doncaster, where the king's force headed by Thomas Howard, the Duke of Norfolk, was outnumbered by three to one. He tried but failed to persuade the Yorkshire nobles and gentry to hand over the traitor, Aske; not wanting any unnecessary bloodshed, Aske persuaded the rebel army to disperse when Norfolk suggested that Henry might pardon the rebels and agree to the calling of a parliament at York. Aske then went to London to explain to Henry the nature of the pilgrims' grievances. They met at Greenwich Palace at Christmas and when Aske blamed Thomas Cromwell, Henry's right-hand man, as being the cause of 7,000 priests having been made homeless by the dissolution of the monasteries, Henry feigned agreement. Having plundered and destroyed religious houses by instigating an Act of Parliament dissolving them and transferring their property to the crown, Cromwell had well earned the nickname, 'Hammer of the Monks'.

Aske was allowed to return home with a promise that the king would visit York, where a parliament and free elections would be held. But in the meantime, another rebellion had broken out in the East Riding over which Aske had no control and he wrote to the king warning him of further impending unrest. It came on 16 January 1537, when Sir Francis Bigod of Mulgrave Castle near Whitby, rose in concert with his tenant, John Hallam, a yeoman from Watton, near Beverley. Fearing that Aske was softening in his will and might even be planning to betray the pilgrims' cause, Bigod's intention was to seize the town of Hull and the royal castle at Scarborough. His force succeeded in occupying Beverley on 18 January, but thanks to Aske's warning, a dawn raid carried out by a Royalist force led by Sir Ralph Ellerker put paid to his plans, which neither Aske nor the people or gentry supported. Bigod managed to escape back to his castle in North Yorkshire, but he was later captured in Cumberland and hanged at Tyburn. The king wrote to Aske thanking him for his action in pacifying Sir Francis Bigod's rising. But his thanks were insincere and Aske's position was now perilous to say the least.

On 24 March, both Aske and Darcy were persuaded to go to London on false assurances of security and in the belief that the king wanted to show his gratitude for the part they had played in helping to prevent the Bigod rebellion. They were arrested upon arrival and tried at Westminster before being sentenced to death for high treason. Aske was taken back to Yorkshire and paraded ignominiously through the towns and country. In July he was hanged in chains at York outside Clifford's tower and butchered in the cruellest manner on a scaffold built specially for the occasion. Until the very end he maintained that both Henry and Cromwell had promised him a pardon and Aske's servant was so distraught at the injustice of it all that he died of grief prior to his master's execution. It turned out that Cromwell had indeed received a letter signed by Aske and Darcy calling on the pilgrims not to join in Bigod's splinter group, but to remain at home. But Cromwell merely construed it as being proof of treason on the grounds that it did not encourage active suppression of the uprising. Three years later, Cromwell would face his own long walk to the executioner's block. Many others from the East Riding would face the executioner's axe in the aftermath of the Pilgrimage of Grace, including holy men from Bridlington, Watton and Warter priories. Gentry such as Sir Thomas Percy – the second son of the fifth Earl of Northumberland, and Sir Robert Constable – the eldest son of Sir Marmaduke Constable of Flamborough, were also found guilty of treason and executed.

Punishment tended, more often than not, to be extremely cruel in what can only be described as a barbaric age. And it was not just meted out to men who fell foul of the law. A woman who suffered an inhuman death for her faith was Margaret Clitherow (1556–1586) who was canonised by the Roman Catholic Church in 1970. She came from a respected family who lived in The Shambles in York (Fig. 14), which is today the most famous and well-preserved medieval street in the city. Her father was Sheriff of York in 1564 and her husband a chamberlain of the city. The problem arose in 1574 when Margaret converted to Roman Catholicism. When it was noticed that she was failing to attend services at her local protestant church, she was imprisoned. In fact, her third child was born in prison. But worse than this, Margaret was hiding Catholic priests who were calling at her home to celebrate mass. Suspecting that her house was under surveillance, she rented another house some distance away. Nonetheless, her home became a refuge for fugitive Catholic priests in the north of England. Tradition has it that the Black Swan Inn at Peaseholme Green was another place where priests and crown agents lodged. Having sent her eldest son abroad to train as a priest, it wasn't long before the authorities were calling on the Clitherow household asking for an explanation. A search of their house revealed a priest hole and resulted in Margaret's arrest on the charge of harbouring Catholic priests. Having refused to plead, she was found guilty at York assizes and executed by crushing, that is to say being stripped naked and laid across a sharp stone and a weight applied above her body until her back broke. When she heard about the affair, and especially the cruel means of execution, Queen Elizabeth I wrote a letter of regret to the citizens of York. And in 2008, a memorial plaque was unveiled at the Micklegate end of the Ouse Bridge where Margaret was executed. There is also a shrine to St Margaret at 35-36, The Shambles, where Margaret lived and where her husband had his butcher's shop.

A son of York, who lived through the same dangerous times as Margaret Clitherow was Guy Fawkes of Gunpowder Plot fame. Born in 1570, he was a member of a group of Roman Catholics who planned to assassinate James I and to proclaim one of the king's younger children as the new (Catholic) monarch. Although James had protected Catholics when he first ascended the throne, it wasn't long before their persecution was re-ignited and 6,000 who refused to attend church were brought before the courts in one year alone. Desperate and with no signs of help from foreign Catholic monarchies, the plotters hired a vacant cellar below the Houses of Parliament where they hid thirty-six barrels of gunpowder. The ringleader and member of the Northamptonshire gentry was Robert Catesby, who found Fawkes a willing conspirator. Not only was his mother's side of the family staunch Catholic, his headmaster at St Peter's School in York came from a family of noted Yorkshire recusants (Pullein 1915). Having served in the Catholic Spanish army and fought against the Protestant Dutch, he had travelled to Spain to seek Catholic support, but without success. No one was more prepared than Fawkes to ignite the gunpowder when the king arrived in the building to open Parliament on 28 July 1605. As fate had it, there was a delay in the opening due to fear of the plague and it was delayed until 5 November 1605. This proved critical because it gave sufficient time for someone who was worried about Catholics being in Parliament at the same time as the king to send an anonymous warning letter. The letter found its way to Robert Cecil, the Earl of Salisbury, who showed it to the king and the tip off led to a search of Westminster Palace. Fawkes was caught red-handed with the stockpile of gunpowder and was summarily tortured. He and the other conspirators were found guilty of high treason and were executed in January the following year. In actual fact, Fawkes cheated the executioner by either falling or jumping from the scaffold before he could be hanged, but his dead body was, nevertheless, quartered and his body parts displayed as a warning to would-be traitors.

A Yorkshire man who managed to escape the persecution of James and sail away on the *Mayflower* in 1620 to become a founder father of Plymouth Colony in America, was William Bradford (1590–1657) who was born in the village of Austerfield, near Doncaster in South Yorkshire. Bradford was a farmer's son who was orphaned at the age of 7 and brought up by two uncles who were also farmers. While still a child, he met fellow *Mayflower* passenger, William Brewster, who was a postmaster and bailiff in a nearby village. Brewster lent him books and engaged him with stories about church reform, to which James I was opposed. Secret meetings were held among a group of reform-minded individuals who began worshipping together and many were eventually arrested and imprisoned or fined – as in Brewster's case. Fearing the worst, the group decided to flee across the North Sea to the Dutch Republic, which was an illegal act at the time. Now aged 18, Bradford went with them, but the ship's captain broke his promise and turned them all over to the authorities. After being imprisoned briefly, the group or congregation as they considered themselves, was finally able to reach Amsterdam by splitting into smaller groups. Within a year they moved to Leiden and in 1617, after ten years in exile, they decided to start a colony in America. In 1620, they left the Dutch Republic aboard the *Speedwell*, before transferring in Southampton to the more seaworthy ship, the *Mayflower*. After two failed attempts, due to problems with the seaworthiness of the *Speedwell*, *Mayflower* finally set sail alone, leaving Plymouth on 6 September 1620 and reaching Cape Cod harbour on 11 November. Now aged 30, Bradford was among those who set out to seek a suitable place for a settlement, finally choosing what became Plymouth Harbour. In April the following year Bradford was chosen as governor of the colony, a position he would hold on-and-off for the rest of his life.

A major issue for sailors navigating the globe up to and including the early part of the eighteenth century was the problem of calculating longitude while at sea. Knowledge of a ship's east-to-west position was critical when approaching land, especially after a long voyage when cumulative errors often led to shipwrecks and a great loss of life. Avoiding such disasters became vital in an era when trade was increasing dramatically around the world. Finding latitude at sea was routine and fairly accurate by 1700, but finding longitude and thus knowing exactly where you were was mostly guesswork.

Astronomers naturally thought the answer lay in observing the skies, while others thought it was in a good seaworthy clock, if one could be found. Brilliant minds of the day, including Sir Isaac Newton and Christiaan Huygens, doubted that such a clock could ever be built. But self-educated carpenter and clockmaker, John Harrison (1693–1776), would prove them wrong. Born in

Foulby near Wakefield, Harrison spent thirty years experimenting and six years of constructing the world's first sea watch or marine chronometer, which was carried aboard a Royal Navy ship on a voyage from Portsmouth to Kingston, Jamaica, on 18 November 1761. His invention not only revolutionised navigation, it greatly increased the safety of long-distance sea travel. Had it been available in 1707, it would have prevented one of the worst naval tragedies in British maritime history, namely, the Isles of Scilly naval disaster in which an English fleet led by Admiral of the Fleet, Sir Cloudesley Shovell, struck rocks and sank with a loss of 2,000 men. It was this shocking news that prompted the British Parliament to sanction a huge reward of £20,000 to solve the longitude problem. Harrison first came up with a sea clock design in 1730, which took him five years to build. During trials it performed well and Harrison was encouraged to develop it further. After five more years of building and testing came his second sea clock in which he discovered a serious flaw, namely, it was aversely affected by the yawing action of a ship. He would spend the next seventeen years working on a third sea clock, which again proved to be unsatisfactory. Eventually, he produced his first sea watch, but despite it working perfectly, it failed to win him the Board of Longitude prize. After a retrial, which involved a vessel sailing from England to Bridgetown, Barbados, the Board eventually offered Harrison an advance of £10,000. In the meantime, however, Harrison decided he had had enough and took his case to the king, who petitioned Parliament. Finally, at the age of 80, he received almost £9,000 for his life-long efforts, but the official award was never made.

Let us now move forward in time to the Stuart dynasty and the unhappy reign of Charles I (1625–1649), of which by far the largest single event was the English Civil War. Although his people warmly welcomed him to the throne, a long quarrel soon ensued between Charles and his parliaments, which was exacerbated by his wife's Catholic friends at court. His favouritism towards Roman Catholicism came at a time when puritanical forces were growing. 'He had not the sense or the knowledge to form a correct estimate of the enormous strength of the new forces that were growing in the nation,' wrote Meiklejohn. 'His wife [the daughter of the king of France], who was one of his advisers, hated the Puritans, and urged him to rule like a French king. Thus, in the first three years of his reign he had managed so that every branch of the nation – the Lords, the Commons, and the People – stood before him in an attitude of hostility.' In short, the power struggle between Charles and Parliament went from bad to worse and a civil war became inevitable.

It would last four long and bloody years. The two sides were roughly divided between the middle classes and tradesmen who supported parliament, and the nobility and peasant class who sided with the king (Delderfield 1970). Power in the north had been delegated by Charles to Thomas Wentworth, one of two new advisers whose sole purpose was to make Charles an absolute monarch. He presided over the Council of the North, which met in York and held boundless power over the northern counties. So much so, that those who held unapproved religious opinions were taken to trial, as were those who spoke ill of the king's policies or failed to bow to his extortion from a variety of illegal means disguised as taxes. Chief among these was so-called 'ship-money', which was imposed at the mere will of Charles without the consent of Parliament, and which had little or nothing to do with ships. His intention was to use it to finance his standing army. When anyone asked for a precedence they were told that the precedence was obedience! The war proper began on 22 August 1642 when Charles raised his standard on a stormy day at Nottingham. The north, together with the west and the counties bordering Wales tended towards Charles and he no doubt expected few problems for enlistment in Yorkshire, but earlier in April he had gone to Hull – the magazine of the north – where the gates to the fortified town were kept firmly shut by Sir John Hotham, Hull's governor. This was a major blow to Charles because the ports of Hull, Bristol, London and Plymouth were estimated to represent two-thirds of England's population and three-quarters of the country's wealth. And the wealthy south-east, which had the most commercial and manufacturing activity, was on the side of Parliament (Meiklejohn). Although the majority of Hull's inhabitants were Royalists, the town had a large arsenal and Hotham had been ordered by Parliament to seize Hull before Charles (who knew that the armouries in London were beyond his reach) arrived for armaments to use against them. Hotham was on the point of changing his mind when Charles appeared once again at the city gate after having collected more soldiers from the nearby town of Beverley. In the event, he was refused entry a second time and the greatly offended Charles declared Hotham a traitor before finally abandoning the siege. An archaeological excavation in the late 1980s revealed the exact location of Hull's Beverley gate and a section of the original town wall is exposed to public view at the Princes Quay end of Whitefriargate.

The first pitched battle of the war took place at Edgehill near Banbury on 23 October 1642, but ended in stalemate. Later that year there were various skirmishes, notably at the bridge over the River Wharfe in Tadcaster. In February the following year, the queen, who had been sent to Holland by Charles in order to sell or pawn the crown jewels to finance the war, returned to Bridlington on the Yorkshire coast with four ships laden with munitions. The next month she set out for Royalist-held York with a convoy of 500 waggons. And in June, 10,000 Royalists marched on Bradford where between 3,000 and 4,000 Parliamentarian troops were stationed. As the town was not sufficiently secure to resist an attack, the smaller Parliamentarian force chose to march towards the approaching Royalists who had reached Adwalton Moor, near Bradford. The Royalists got the upper hand in the resulting clash, leaving the Parliamentarians with only Hull and Wressle castle as its sole strongholds in the north. By the late summer, Hull had become the focus of a second Royalist attack. On 28 August the Earl of Newcastle reached Beverley with 16,000 men and sacked the town, which had been previously occupied by a far inferior Parliamentarian force led by Sir Thomas Fairfax. This latter force had retreated to Hull, which itself came under siege four days later. The siege lasted almost six weeks, but after constant harrying by Parliamentarian forces, the besieging Royalist force was eventually beaten off and the Royalist magazine at Cottingham blown up. Lord Fairfax finally rode out of Hull on 11 October (Neave 1996).

If 1643 had been a good year for the Royalists, 1644 would be a turning point for the Parliamentarians. They had been gaining territory in a number of raids, notably in Bradford, Bridlington and Whitby, which were all captured. Stamford Bridge was taken in April, as was the Royalist headquarters at Selby, but not until after bitter fighting. In May, the castles at Buttercrambe and Cawood, and the fort at Airemouth, Airmyn were captured (Neave 1996). This meant that half of the Royalist forces in Yorkshire had now been defeated and Royalist held York, England's northern capital, which in April had been under siege and in June relieved by Prince Rupert, was now under threat from the huge Scottish-parliamentary army that had encircled it. On 2 July 1644, 20,000 Scottish troops entered the fray at the request of the English Parliament and marched to Marston Moor, near York, where they joined Parliamentary forces. In total, 34,000 men and 14,000 horses were deployed in battle, which commenced that same evening. A particularly bloody encounter ensued, which ended in the loss of 4,500 lives, but may have been nearer to twice that amount. A further 1,500 Royalists were captured, effectively destroying the northern Royalist army. After the victory at Marston Moor, Cromwell jubilantly proclaimed the superiority of Parliamentarian forces when he proclaimed, 'We never charged, but we routed the enemy. The left wing, which I commanded, being our own horse, saving a few Scots in our rear, beat all the Prince's horse. God made them stubble to our swords.' Two weeks later Royalist York was surrendered, leaving Royalist-held garrisons only at Bolton, Helmsley, Knaresborough, Pontefract, Sandal, Scarborough and Skipton. Parliament was now able to concentrate its forces in the south.

All that remains at Marston Moor as a reminder of what arguably became England's most bloody battle is a simple stone memorial. But the mass graves of the thousands who died here were visible right up to the start of the nineteenth century. The survivors made their painful way towards York where a beacon was lit each night. For centuries this flame had been a guiding light for those passing through the Forest of Galtres and the tradition of a burning lantern is maintained to this day. In her book about the Yorkshire Ouse, Alison Waite writes:

> Thus, following the tortured route of those maimed men of war, the modern traveller too can be guided past now tranquil Ouse-side villages to the city. It is peculiar that these bastions

of civilised peace witnessed the events of such a devastating, powerful and far-reaching part of English history yet these villages seem somehow untouched.... The sense of times past hangs heavy in the mists that shroud the plain and the ghosts of the thousands who died linger on the border of Wilstrop Wood.

There followed a second battle of Newbury in October 1644, the outcome of which was indecisive, but at the Battle of Naseby, near Northampton in June 1645, Cromwell's New Model Army scored a decisive victory in which the Royalists suffered 6,000 casualties and from which Charles's army never recovered. 'The royal reserve fled; the battle was over; and the war was ended at a blow,' wrote Meiklejohn.

The artillery, the baggage, and even the royal papers fell into the hands of the conquerors; and Charles fled for safety and for fresh forces into Wales. The most precious spoil of the day was the king's cabinet, which when opened, disclosed secrets which more injured his cause than any victory of his enemies. Foreign princes were asked to send their soldiers to conquer rebel England. The dreaded Papists were to be freed from every restraint on the condition of such assistance (Knight).

Charles would eventually surrender himself to the Scottish army at Newark and was duly handed over to Parliament. He stood trial in January 1649 and was executed later that month.

The gentry were, strangely, split down the middle in the Civil War, especially in the East Riding, with a few remaining neutral or undecided. The leading Catholic families were all Royalists, and one of their most skilled cavalry commanders was Sir Marmaduke Langdale of Holme-upon-Spalding-Moor. One of the leading Parliamentarians was Sir William Constable, who, together with Colonel John Alured of Hull, would sign Charles I's death warrant. But families were also divided in their loyalties and some would even change sides. Sir Matthew Boynton of Barmston, for instance, held

Scarborough castle for Parliamentarians from 1645 until his death in 1647. But his second son, also called Matthew, first held the castle for the Parliamentarians and then for the king. And it was he who captured Sir John Hotham in Beverley after finding correspondence between him and his son linking them with the Royalists and for which they were executed in 1645. Hotham had earlier refused Charles entry into Hull prior to the conflict. (Neave 1996)

This seems as good a place as any to mention a few facts about the ancient market town of Beverley in the East Riding, which happens to be my birth place and is much older than the average visitor might think. Modern dating methods have shown that charcoal fragments recovered from a ditch at a former Knights Hospitallers preceptory site in the town date back to the start of the third millennium BC, while a stake and wattle fence found in the town date back to the first millennium BC. Neolithic and Bronze Age finds have also been recovered, as have those dating from Roman times suggesting that at least one farmstead stood at the northern end of what is now Beverley (Evans 1996). One certain fact is that St John of Beverley founded a monastery here in the early eighth century. This was the first recorded settlement around which the town was built in the years following the Norman conquest. The original attraction, however, may have been that the relatively high ground offered the only reasonably dry crossing point of the Hull valley. The town's closeness to the River Hull and therefore easy access for water-borne traffic was key to the further economic success and growth of the town, which developed into a hub for shipment of wares, such as wool, textiles and hides that the town's tradespeople became expert at processing. The abundance of clay in the area played no small part in the town's growth, as did the large numbers of pilgrims visiting the shrine of St John (Evans 1996). We learn from the writings of an early twelfth-century Beverley priest that Athelstan (AD 925–940), the grandson of Alfred the Great, visited the shrine in AD 973 to pray on his way north to fight the Scots. In thanks for his victory, he bestowed on the minster great privileges, including the right of sanctuary. Beverley Minster now stands on the site of the original shrine, but it was severely damaged by fire in 1188. Despite being rebuilt, most of the building came down when the central tower collapsed in or around 1219 and it would take a further 200 years to complete the existing building, which became celebrated as one of the country's finest examples of Early English architecture. The parish churches of St Mary's and St Nicholas were built around the middle of the twelfth century to administer to the needs of an expanding population and the town's defences also date from this period. Beverley is known never to have been completely encircled by defences, but there were at least three entrances to the medieval town, of which only the North Bar has weathered the ravages of time. In 1334 Beverley was among the top twenty towns in England in terms of the number of taxpayers, and in 1377 it had risen to tenth position (Dyer 1991). By 1599 it was described as being very poor and greatly depopulated with many houses decayed and uninhabited (Miller et al 1982). This decline is thought to have been linked with the diminishing wool trade and the textile industry, as well as the Dissolution of the Monasteries. Loss of privileges, such as the rights of sanctuary in 1540, would have also impacted the town, as would the plague, which struck in 1604 and 1610. The low point in the town's fortunes and development probably came with the English Civil War in 1643. In the late seventeenth century the scholar and cleric, Edmund Gibson, saw a marked improvement in its buildings, as did the daughter of an English Civil War Parliamentarian Army colonel, who in 1697 observed how Beverley was a fine town for its size with quite tall new buildings. This was in complete contrast to when the antiquary, John Leland, first saw the town in 1540 and described it as being 'much decayid' (Woodward 1985). Beverley would continue to develop into the administrative capital of the East Riding.

The famed and much travelled poet and politician Andrew Marvell lived during this time. Born in the East Riding village of Winestead in 1621, he was the son of a clergyman who moved to Hull where he was attached to the Holy Trinity Church (now Hull Minster). Marvell attended Hull Grammar School and at the age of 13 went to study at Trinity College, Cambridge. During the English Civil War he travelled on the continent and worked as a tutor until his return to England in 1647. He then served as a private tutor to the daughter of the Lord General Thomas Fairfax, the former commander of the Parliamentarian army, during which time he lived at Nun Appleton Hall, near York. He wrote several poems in praise of Cromwell, who was by this time was Lord Protector of England. He also befriended the poet and man of letters, John Milton, with whom he worked together as Latin secretary to Cromwell's Council of State. By 1654, Milton had become totally blind and he dictated his work to Marvell, who copied it out for him, among others. In 1659, the year after Cromwell's death, Marvell was elected as a member of parliament for Hull and is known to have sat in the House of Commons between 1659 until his death in 1678. After the Restoration in May 1660, he wrote political verse satires and was instrumental in obtaining Milton's release from prison.

Religious fervour became intense during the seventeenth century, culminating in what became known as the Popish Plot – a supposed Catholic conspiracy to kill Charles II that was fabricated by a renegade priest and self-styled Protestant champion called Titus Oates who called himself the 'Saviour of the Nation'. Between 1678 and 1681 the Popish Plot led to anti-Catholic hysteria in England and Scotland. Oats had indeed studied at a Jesuit seminary, but had been expelled, just as he had been from school and from the Navy. His accusations, which were set out in a declaration titled, 'True and Exact Narrative of the Horrid Plot and Conspiracy of the Popish Party against the Life of His Sacred Majesty, the Government and the Protestant Religion, etc. published by the Order of the Right Honorable the Lords Spiritual and Temporal in Parliament assembled', were described as being 'clumsy, puerile, ill-written, disjointed libels, hardly worth notice but for the frenzied anger they aroused'. The chief accusation told of a design to assassinate the king, upon which 'the capital and the whole nation were mad with hatred and fear,' wrote the historian and politician, Thomas Macaulay. Many went into hiding and fifty-seven Jesuits died in prison or on the scaffold. One such person was the 82-year-old Catholic priest, Nicholas Postgate (1596–1679) of Egton, North Yorkshire, who was carrying out a private baptism at Little Beck near Whitby when he was arrested. The story goes that the person who arrested him bore a grudge against Catholics and blamed them for the murder of his master, who was a prominent Protestant magistrate in London. Postgate was tried and found guilty of being nothing more than a Roman Catholic priest. He was hung, disembowelled and quartered at Knavesmire in York. Two years later, Oats would be discredited, heavily fined and imprisoned. On the accession of James II, he was retried and found guilty of perjury before being pilloried and imprisoned for life. Lucky to have escaped with his life after having been the cause of so many deaths, Oats was to be taken from prison on five days every year and whipped through the streets of London. The infamous Judge Jeffries, the 'Hanging Judge', only regretted that the death penalty could not be imposed for perjury at that time. However, upon the accession of the Protestant King, William of Orange, Oats would be shown uncommon mercy and pardoned after serving just three years of his sentence. Upon release from prison and with his reputation in tatters, he lived in obscurity until the age of 55. Nicholas Postgate, on the other hand, would become revered as 'The Martyr of the Moors'.

Religious persecution began again during the reign of James II (1685–1688). As the brother of Charles II, he had openly embraced Catholicism in 1673. This had made him greatly unpopular due to the violent anti-Catholic sentiments in the wake of the Popish Plot. So much so, that attempts were made to exclude him from the succession and he was persuaded by Charles to go abroad. When James II finally acceded to the throne, however, it was met within six months by a rebellion of Protestant adherents to James, the Duke of Monmouth. He was subsequently captured and executed, but in the aftermath of the uprising, there were well over 200 executions and many more either died in prison, were fined, flogged or transported for life. In December 1688, James vacated the throne and fled to France, dropping the great seal of the kingdom into the River Thames on his way. The strong religious sentiment relating to this tragic period continued in Hull, where in 1688 the residence of the deputy-governor of Hull [now Ye Olde White Harte public house] was the location of the meeting to plot the overthrow of the town's Catholic governor. He had been appointed by James II following the arrival of William of Orange in

England in November 1688, an event that was long commemorated as 'Town Taking Day'.

In the mid-eighteenth century there was again unrest in Yorkshire, as well as in several other counties, as part of what became known as The Militia Act Riots. These were caused by revisions to the Militia Acts, which were hurriedly passed by Parliament in response to the threat of a French invasion during the Seven Years' War. Counties were responsible for raising a militia force for which officers were appointed from among the property-owning class. All able-bodied men of a parish aged from 18 to 50 were eligible, and could opt out if they wished, as long as they were able to nominate someone who was willing to serve in their place. The alternative was to be fined the not inconsiderable sum of £10. The main objection was from the poorer classes, who could not only ill-afford a £10 fine, but were also unable to abandon their jobs and families for up to three years while they served in the militia (Western 1965). This unreasonable piece of legislation caused uproar throughout the shire, but especially in the East Riding. 'In September 1757, the East Riding community experienced what was probably its most serious period of unrest since the Pilgrimage of Grace,' wrote Neave. 'Day after day hundreds of men, women and children, armed with guns, swords, pitchforks and scythes, gathered at the houses of gentry, clergy and law officers, threatening to pull the buildings down unless a stop was put to the new Militia Act.' Incidents were recorded from Winestead in Holderness, where Sir Robert Hilyard's residence was threatened, to Hedon, Cottingham, Beverley, Pocklington and beyond. 'At Birdsall the High Sheriff was visited by an armed mob from forty townships numbering, he claimed, 3,000,' continued Neve. 'Six hundred rioters surrounded the hall at Howsham, some of whom went on to visit the rectors of Settrington and Scrayingham. About 1,000 gathered at Hunmanby Hall where they broke all the windows before going on to Buckton Hall.' On 15 September, 2,000 rioters from North Yorkshire pulled down an inn in York where a meeting of deputy lieutenants was being held. This was the last recorded disturbance and by mid-September the riots had ended. In March the following year more than one hundred people were tried at York Assizes for their participation, the vast majority being from the East Riding. Forty were found guilty and received mere prison sentences, but four were singled out as ringleaders and found guilty of high treason. Their penalty was hanging, being cut down while still alive and then being drawn and quartered. In the event, only one offender, a Bridlington man, paid the ultimate price and was sent to the gallows (Neave 1996).

We now fast-forward to the time of George III, whose reign was exceptionally long (1760–1820) if not entirely happy. Together with Lord North, the British Prime Minister (1770–1782), he presided over the loss the American colonies during the American War of Independence, but in 1783 he resigned much of his personal power. He would later become both blind and insane. It was during the American War of Independence that the conflict came alarmingly close to Yorkshire shores in the shape of an attack on British ships by Scottish-born John Paul Jones and his American warship the *Bonhomme Richard*. A common pirate in the eyes of the British Admiralty, Jones rose in notoriety on 23 September 1779 in a naval engagement that was fought off Flamborough Head (Fig. 15). During the action Jones attacked a Baltic merchant convoy under the protection of HMS *Serapis*, a fifty-gun frigate, and the twenty-two-gun vessel *Countess of Scarborough*. In the ensuing struggle there were heavy casualties on both sides and just when the British appeared to be gaining the upper hand, Jones used grappling irons to capture HMS *Serapis* and lash the two ships together. The ploy was devastating to the British ship's manoeuvrability and therefore the effectiveness of her gun power; once she was boarded, the larger crew of the American warship was eventually able to beat the British in hand-to-hand fighting. Four hours after the start of the engagement, another ship from Jones's convoy joined the fray and the British surrendered, but nothing could save the burning and badly damaged *Bonhomme Richard* from slipping beneath the waves.

Triumphant in his capture of a British ship of the line, Jones sailed her to the Dutch coast where she was repaired for further action. And although Jones had lost his own ship, his success in the Battle of Flamborough Head helped to convince the French to support the American colonies in their fight for independence.

The wreck of the *Bonhomme Richard* was only recently discovered by a Harrogate-based archaeology firm close to the beach at Filey, while cannon ball supposed to have been fired by Jones was found in a field near Rowlston Hall, between Hornsea and Mappleton on the East Yorkshire coast. As a boy I frequented a nearby cottage and remember the inscrutable hall, which was surrounded by trees and often enshrouded in a sea roke that made its appearance even more mysterious. At the time of the naval engagement off Flamborough Head, the hall was owned William Brough Esquire, Marshal of the High Court of Admiralty, who was entrusted with the fight against piracy at the time and it is thought that Jones fired the shot as a mark of his contempt. In 1763, the subject of Admiralty courts had become a burning issue between the British and the colonies, as they were given jurisdiction over a number of laws affecting the colonies. For instance, the courts could try a case anywhere in the British Empire and cases against New York or Boston merchants were frequently heard in Nova Scotia and sometimes even in England. Moreover, judges decided the outcome of a trial rather than a jury. One high-profile trial that William Brough presided over was that of Admiral John Byng who was found guilty and executed in 1757 for failing to relieve the British naval base on the island of Minorca from a French siege. On the eve of the Seven Years' War with France (1756–63), Byng had been sent with an inadequate force to defend the island, but arrived too late to prevent the landing of a French force that was already besieging the British base at Fort St Philip. Seeing the futility of the situation, Byng broke off his engagement with the French and returned to Gibraltar. Neither the British Parliament nor the Admiralty were enthralled with this abject failure and Byng was court-martialled on his own flagship in Portsmouth harbour. Found guilty of neglect of duty, he was executed by a firing squad of marines (Encyclopaedia Britannica).

Meanwhile, twenty years of war had caused widespread misery and discontent in the country, not to mention having trebled the national debt. Hundreds of thousands of poor people were starving, thousands of former soldiers and sailors were without work, and to make matters worse, the lack of labour during the war had led to the invention of new machinery, which had thrown thousands more out of work. It seemed as though the war years had simply enriched those with either land or money, while the poor had become even poorer. Riots ensued and a new term entered into the English language, namely, 'Luddism'. Named after the fictional character, Ned Ludd, who became symbolic for the destruction of machinery after breaking two mechanical knitting machines in a fit of rage, Luddites roamed the country breaking, burning and pillaging in industrial towns. The trouble began in Nottinghamshire in November 1811, but was quickly followed by similar unrest in the West Riding of Yorkshire early in 1812. Things came to a head when three Luddites were arrested after ambushing and shooting a mill owner at Crosland Moor in Huddersfield. There was a further attack at a mill near Cleckheaton, to the south of Bradford and sixty men were charged with various crimes in connection with Luddite activities, although thirty were eventually acquitted due to lack of evidence. The law already dealt severely with such matters (fourteen years' transportation) with the intention of dissuading others from joining the fray. However, an emergency Bill was passed that made Luddism a capital offence and in 1812, sixteen of their number were tried and hanged in York (Meiklejohn).

During the nineteenth century and especially during the reign of Queen Victoria, Britain entered an age of supremacy and grew exponentially in terms of material prosperity and economic power. Towards the end of Victoria's reign it led the world in industry, manufacturing and commerce, and supplied more than a third of the world's shipping. In 1874, the value of her export trade was equal to that of France, Germany, Italy and the USA put together. Between 1800 and 1890 the British Empire more than doubled in size to cover in excess of one-seventh of the globe and it was home to about one fourth of the world's population. Invasion and conflict seemed a very long way from our shores. And it was for a short period. But times were changing and a conflict to top all conflicts was much nearer than anyone could have imagined.

Chapter 11

Yorkshire at War

When Leeds (Kirkstall) born aviation pioneer, Robert Blackburn (1885–1955), flew his first aircraft from the beach at Filey in 1909, little could he have realised the scale of the conflict into which the world would shortly be plunged. His second aircraft, the Blackburn Type D (1912) single-engine monoplane, is preserved in flying condition by the Shuttleworth Collection at Old Warden in Bedfordshire and is the oldest British-built aircraft in existence. The Blackburn Aircraft Company (later the Blackburn Aeroplane & Motor Company) initially built aircraft at the Olympia works in Leeds before later opening a new factory at Brough in the East Riding, where there was easy access to the Humber foreshore for launching and testing floatplanes. Seeing an opportunity to expand his business, Robert started offering half-hourly flights between Leeds and Bradford, which was the first scheduled air service in the country. In 1919 he founded the North Sea Aerial Navigation Company, which operated a passenger and cargo service from Leeds Roundhay Park Aerodrome to London, Hounslow, and later on to Amsterdam. With the closure of Roundhay Aerodrome in 1920, the Leeds factory closed entirely and during the Second World War, Battle of Britain fighter pilots honed their skills at Brough aerodrome's flight training school. After the war the company changed its name to Blackburn & General Aircraft Limited and would go on to produce aeroplanes of almost every type. My first proper job was at Brough, where I had a grandstand view over the airfield. During lunch breaks on fine summer days, Bernard Watson, the head of Flight Test, would treat us to aerobatic displays in a Blackburn B2 biplane (Fig. 16), which appeared at air shows and events throughout the UK and is shown flying over Yorkshire in 1960. Bernard was one of two pilots aboard the Blackburn NA39 Buccaneer on its maiden flight from Holme-upon-Spalding-Moor to RAE Bedford on 30 April 1958 (Fig. 17). The Buccaneer was the last aircraft to bear the Blackburn name and with the cancellation of the TSR2 project also became Britain's last dedicated bomber. Standing next to Bernard in the photograph is Chief Test Pilot, Derek Whitehead.

The name of Hull-born pioneering aviator, Amy Johnson (1903–1941), should be mentioned at this point. The eldest of four daughters of a Hull fish merchant, she was introduced to flying as a hobby after graduating from Sheffield University. In 1929 she was awarded her pilot's licence and ground engineer's licence – the latter being the first ever to be awarded to a British woman. The following year she achieved worldwide recognition by becoming the first woman to fly solo from England to Australia, a distance of 11,000 miles, which she achieved in her Gipsy Moth aircraft. Other records were set to tumble. In July 1931, she and her co-pilot became the first aviators to fly in a single day from London to Moscow, a distance of 1,760 miles. They continued to Tokyo to set a record time for a flight from Britain to Japan. The following year she set a solo record for flying from London to Cape Town and a year later she was again in Australia flying with her husband non-stop to New York. It was during this flight that her aircraft ran out of fuel and crash-landed. Despite being injured, both she and her husband soon recovered and received a ticker-tape welcome in New York. More records tumbled: in 1934 the fastest flight ever to India from Britain, and in 1936 the fastest-ever flight to South Africa from Britain. But that was the last of her record-breaking flights. War intervened and in January 1941, while delivering a training aircraft for the RAF from Prestwick aerodrome to RAF Kidlington near Oxford, she lost her bearings in adverse weather conditions and ran out of fuel. Believed to have bailed out over the Thames Estuary, crewmen of a Royal Navy barrage balloon ship spotted a descending parachutist enter the water and called for help. Unfortunately there was a heavy sea and a strong tide, and visibility was poor due to falling snow. Notwithstanding this, the commander of the barrage balloon ship risked his own life by diving into the water in an attempted rescue. It failed and he later died in hospital (*The Times* 1941). Amy's body was never recovered, but the son of a crewman stated that Amy was drawn towards the ship's propellers, although the crewman did not see this with his own eyes (*The Daily Telegraph* 2016). In 1958, Amy's family donated a collection of souvenirs and memorabilia to Sewerby Hall near Bridlington, where a dedicated Amy Johnson room is open to the public. To commemorate her life and achievements, a statue of Amy was unveiled in 1974 in Prospect Street, Hull; on the 75th anniversary of her death, further statues were unveiled close to Amy's childhood home near Hawthorne Avenue, Hull, and at Herne Bay on the Kent coast, close to where she was last seen alive.

Many of Yorkshire's sons and daughters would sacrifice their lives during both the First and Second World War and there is hardly a village or town in the county without a memorial bearing testimony to the fact. The majority of young men waited for conscription into the armed services, but there was no shortage of volunteers waiting in line to serve their king and country. The recruitment poster by Lucy E. Kemp-Welch (Fig. 18) suggests the emotions that must have been awakened by what happened on 16 December 1914 when the German Navy decided to attack a number of ports in the northeast of England. Scarborough and Whitby were included in the attacks, which came as a complete surprise and resulted in the death of 137 people in addition to extensive collateral damage. There were 592 casualties in total and the public reacted with outrage, not simply because the German attacks, after all the two countries were at war, but the fact that many of the casualties were civilians. The Royal Navy also came in for criticism because what was regarded as the mightiest fleet afloat was expected to have been able to prevent the Germans simply crossing the North Sea and taking pot-shots at our towns. In fact, the Germans had sent a submarine to check out the coastal defences beforehand and it reported an absence of minefields and other deterrents that might hinder an attack. The bombardment, which was carried out by two battle cruisers, scored hits on the castle in Scarborough, the Grand Hotel, three churches and various other properties, after which it moved on to Whitby, where various buildings in the town, including a coastguard station and the abbey, were hit. German ships then attacked the more substantial port of Hartlepool before shore batteries realised what was happening and returned fire. But the ships were gone before they could sustain any serious damage. Apart from the considerable alarm caused among the largely civilian populations, the raid resulted in the first death of a British soldier on English soil during the Great War. Eight German sailors were killed and twelve wounded (Massie 2004).

When the First World War broke out, Henry Herbert Asquith, Earl of Oxford and Asquith (1852–1928) was the British prime minister. Born in the market town of Morley (West Riding), into an old, middle-class, Yorkshire family associated with the wool trade, Asquith trained as a barrister and developed a penchant for debate at Oxford University, where he aired his liberal views. He also wrote regularly for *The Spectator* magazine, which reflected his liberal outlook and expressed his opinions on topics that were much debated at that time, including British imperialism, the union of Great Britain and Ireland, and female suffrage. In 1886 he became a liberal MP and six years later, aged only 39 and without ever having been a junior minister, he was appointed Home Secretary in Gladstone's Cabinet. For a decade following the 1895 general election, the Liberals were out of office, but opportunity knocked in 1905 when the leader of the Conservative government, Arthur Balfour, resigned without seeking re-election. King Edward VII invited the Liberals to form a minority government in which Asquith was made Chancellor of the Exchequer. In 1908, he succeeded as prime minister. But in the election year of 1910, he was left as the head of a minority government with major issues to address, including Irish home rule. In what were far from stable times, a crisis arose in 1914 when Asquith was compelled to declare war on Germany and call for national mobilisation. A year later, when the war effort was not going to plan, he was forced into a coalition government in which the three ruling parties could only agree to disagree. Unable to bring harmony to the government, he was succeeded by his War Secretary, David Lloyd George. The political scene changed in the years following the war and after 1922 the Liberals would never hold office again. Asquith was created the Earl of Oxford and Asquith in 1925 and with his life's work over he slipped quietly into retirement. Historians are generally divided when summing him up. One said: 'A great head of government in peacetime, by the end of 1916 he was in a general state of decline, his obvious defects as a war leader exposed' (Grigg 1985). Another disagreed: 'His achievements are sufficiently impressive to earn him a place as one of the outstanding figures of the Great War,' (Cassar 1994). But one contemporary opponent of his paid this tribute, 'A statesman who rendered great service to his country at a time when no other living Englishman could have done what he did,' (Lord Birkenhead 1924). Beyond his role as British prime minister, Asquith is celebrated for his role in creating the modern British welfare state.

Another famous Yorkshire son who experienced the horror of war on the front line was John Boynton Priestley (1894–1984), the novelist, playwright, scriptwriter, social commentator and broadcaster. Born in Bradford, Priestly attended a local grammar school, but left aged 16 to work for a local wool firm. He wrote newspaper articles at night and drew on memories of his hometown in many of the works he wrote. During the First World War he saw active service in France, where he was badly wounded by mortar fire. After a long period of convalescence he returned to France but fell victim to a gas attack; after demobilisation went to study in Cambridge. By the age of 30 he had become a renowned essayist and critic, but true national fame came with his award-winning novel, *The Good Companions* (1929). This was followed by another novel, *Angel Pavement* (1930), which further established him as a successful novelist. Equally well known as a dramatist whose many plays would entertain packed London West-End theatres, his best-known play was *An Inspector Calls* (1945). During the Second World War he turned to broadcasting and had a regular Sunday-night slot that attracted millions of listeners to the BBC. It was said that only Winston Churchill was more popular than Priestly in the months following the evacuation at Dunkirk (Addison 2011). His broadcasts were considered to have influenced the politics of the period and helped the Labour Party gain its landslide victory in the 1945 general election. One of Priestly's favourite places was the village of Hubberholme in Upper Wharfedale, which he described as the smallest, pleasantest place in the world. In 1970, he was awarded the title of honorary Doctor of Letters by Bradford University, where the library that he opened in 1975 bears his name to this day.

His statue stands in front of the National Science and Media Museum in Bradford.

In little over twenty years since the end of the First World War, it would be the turn of another British prime minister, Neville Chamberlain, to find himself in the unenviable position of declaring war on Germany. Key among the many talented people who contributed to shortening the conflict was the inventor, Donald Coleman Bailey (1901–1985), a Yorkshire engineer who was knighted in 1946 for his design of the transportable Bailey Bridge. Field Marshal Bernard Montgomery himself acknowledged the bridge as having speeded up the Allied advance through Europe. Meanwhile, living and teaching in Hull during the first part of the Second World War was the eminent scientist, author and broadcaster, Jacob Bronowski (1908–1974), who taught mathematics at University College Hull from 1934 to 1942. He contributed to the war effort by performing special services, for instance, developing mathematical approaches to bombing strategy for RAF Bomber Command. At the end of the war he visited Japan to study the effects of the atomic bombs that were unleashed over Hiroshima and Nagasaki, and to figure out the implications for future UK civil defence (Gillet & MacMahon 1980). He was joint author of a secret report for the British Mission to Japan on the effects of the atomic bombs that were exploded, but is perhaps remembered most for the broad public acclaim following his wonderful thirteen-part BBC television series, *The Ascent of Man*, which was compulsory viewing for many millions of viewers in 1973.

It would be easy to go on and on about inspirational people with Yorkshire connections who made their mark when it mattered most to the nation, but their stories will have to wait until another day and perhaps another book. We have, therefore, reached the end of our journey through Yorkshire in time, which I hope has given an insight into how the county's landscape, towns and people have been impacted and indeed shaped over the millennia by invasions, the imposition of various different cultures, and exposure to the many conflicts that have taken place in the county. In her book *Grit*, the psychologist Angela Duckworth explains that whereas there is no single gene for 'grit', or indeed any other psychological trait, it is influenced by genes and experience. And there is a correlation with age: one study showed that the grittiest adults were in their sixties or older, with the least gritty being in their twenties. An explanation for this is that life experiences change personality and the effects of even small environmental differences, or genetic ones, are multiplied socially through culture. 'Some believe that grit is forged in the crucible of adversity,' wrote Duckworth, 'but others are quick to paraphrase Nietzsche: "What doesn't kill you makes you stronger."' So, which is it? Nurture or nature? Findings show that 'grit' paragons can generally point to others in their lives who have been timely examples to them in terms of aiming high. Personally, I like to think that this, rather than simply adversity, is the key to explaining Yorkshire grit.

Bibliography

Barber, Richard, *Henry Plantagenet – A Biography of Henry II of England* (Purnell, London 1964)

Baring Gould, S., 'Eric Bloodaxe in York', (*The Yorkshire Archaeological Journal*, Vol. 22, 1913), p. 241–252

Barley, M.W., 'Rural East Yorkshire', (*A Guide to the History of the East Riding*, University College Hull, 1939)

Billings, Malcolm, *The English – The Making of a Nation from 430–1700* (BBC Books, London, 1991)

Bilson, John, 'Some notes on St Mary's Church, Hull', (*The Yorkshire Archaeological Journal*, Vol. 24, 1913), p. 275–285

Binns, A.L., *The Viking Century in East Yorkshire* (East Yorkshire Local History Society, Beverley, 1963)

Boyle, J.R., *The Danes in the East Riding* (William Andrews and Co., Hull & London, 1895)

Brooks, F.W., *Domesday and the East Riding*, (East Yorkshire Local History Society, Beverley, 1966)

Brooks, F.W., 'The Beginnings of the East Yorkshire Towns', (*A Guide to the History of the East Riding*, University College Hull, 1939)

Burke, John, *Roman England* (Artus Books, London, 1983), p. 109

Catt, J.A., 'Geology and Relief", *Humber Prespectives* (Hull University Press, 1990), p. 13–25

Clunn, Tony, *In Quest of the Lost Legions (Minerva Press*, 1999)

Creighton, J., 'The Humber Frontier in the First Century AD', *Humber Perspectives* (Hull University Press, 1990), p. 182–197

De Boer, George, 'The History of Spurn Point', *An Historical Atlas of East Yorkshire* (The University of Hull Press, 1996), p. 8 and 9

Delderfield, Eric, *Kings and Queens of England and Great Britain* (David & Charles Ltd., Newton Abbot, 1966)

English, Barbara, *The Lords of Holderness 1086–1260 – A Study in Feudal Society* (Oxford University Press, 1979)

Evans, D.H., 'The Archaeology of Beverley', *Humber Perspectives* (Hull University Press, 1990), p. 269–281

Evans, D.H., 'Medieval Beverley', *An Historical Atlas of East Yorkshire* (The University of Hull Press, 1996), p. 40

Flenley, J.R., *'The Meres of Holderness'*, (East Yorkshire Field Guide, 1987)

Garlick, Tom, *Roman Yorkshire* (Dalesman Books, 1988)

Gillett, Edward and MacMahon, Kenneth, *A History of Hull* (For University of Hull by Oxford University Press, 1980)

Gilbertson, D.D., 'The Holderness Meres: stratigraphy, archaeology and environment', *Humberside Perspectives* (Hull University Press, 1990), p. 89–99

Hawkes, Jacquetta, *The Shell Guide to British Archaeology* (Michael Joseph, London, 1986)

Haughton, Christine and Powlesland, Dominic, *West Heslerton – the Anglian Cemetery*, (English heritage, 1999)

Jenkins, Simon, *A Short History of England* (Profile Books Ltd., London, 2012)

Kenchington, Richard, *The Derwent Way* (Dalesman Books, 1978)

Kitson Clark, Mary, 'Roman East Yorkshire', (*A Guide to the History of the East Riding*, University College Hull, 1939)

Knowles, G.C., 'The Humber and its People during the Medieval Period', *Humberside Perspectives* (Hull University Press, 1990), p. 357–370

McElwee, William, *History of England* (The English Universities Press Ltd., 1960)

McGrail, S., 'Early Boats of the Humber Basin', *Humberside Perspectives* (Hull University Press, 1990), p. 109–128

Mead, Harry, 'Yorkshire's Lost Lakeland', Yorkshire Journal No. 38 (Smith Settle Ltd., Ottley, 2002) p. 5–11

MeikleJohn, J.M.D, *A New History of England and Great Britain* (Alfred M. Holden, London, 1897)

Millett, M., 'Iron-Age and Romano-British Dettlement in the Southern Vale of York and beyond', *Humberside Perspectives* (Hull University Press, 1990) p. 347–354

Melton, Nigel; Montgomery, Janet and Knusel, Christopher, *'Gristhorpe Man – A Life and Death in the Bronze Age'* (Oxbow 2013)

Neave, David, 'Post-Medieval Beverley', *Humberside Perspectives* (Hull University Press, 1990), p. 283–303

Neave, David, 'The Pilgrimage of Grace', *An Historical Atlas of East Yorkshire* (The Hull University Press, 1996), p. 120

Neave, David, 'The Civil War in the East Riding', *An Historical Atlas of East Yorkshire* (The Hull University Press, 1996), p. 122

Neave, David, 'Anti-Militia Riots: 1757', *An Historical Atlas of East Yorkshire* (The Hull University Press, 1996), p. 124

Neave, Susan, 'Beverley in the Eighteenth and nineteenth Centuries', *An Historical Atlas of East Yorkshire* (The Hull University Press, 1996), p. 42

Neave, Susan, 'Deserted Settlements', *An Historical Atlas of East Yorkshire* (The Hull University Press, 1996), p. 54

Neave, Susan, 'Medieval Religious Houses', *An Historical Atlas of East Yorkshire* (The Hull University Press, 1996), p. 104

Noble, M.K., 'Market Towns of the Humber North Bank 1700-1850', *Humberside Perspectives* (Hull University Press, 1990), p. 307–319

Noble, Margaret, 'Markets and Fairs', *An Historical Atlas of East Yorkshire* (The Hull University Press, 1996), p. 76

North, J., 'The History of the Humber Crossing', *Humberside Perspectives* (Hull University Press, 1990), p. 406–429

North, J., 'Development of the Humber Region during the Nineteenth and Twentieth Centuries', *Humber Perspectives* (Hull University Press, 1990) p. 422–435

Palgrave, Francis, *History of the Anglo-Saxons* (William Tegg & Co., London, 1876)

Palliser, D.M., 'Markets and Towns in the Middle Ages, *An Historical Atlas of East Yorkshire* (The Hull University Press, 1996), p. 74

Pethick, J.S., 'The Humber Estuary', *Humber Perspectives* (Hull University Press, 1990), p. 54–66

Pye, Michael, *The Edge of the World: How the North Sea Made Us* (Penguin Books Ltd., London, 2014)

Richmond, I.A. 'The Four Roman Camps at Cawthorn in the North Riding of Yorkshire', (*Archaeological Journal* 89, 1932) p. 17–78

Ross, Charles, *Edward IV* (Book Club Associates with Eyre Methuen Ltd., 1975)

Ross, Charles, *The Wars of the Roses* (Thames and Hudson, London, 1976)

Sheppard, Thomas, *The Lost Towns of the Yorkshire Coast* (A. Brown & Sons, London, 1912)

Sheppard, Thomas, 'Prehistoric East Yorkshire' (*A Guide to the History of the East Riding*, University College Hull, 1939)

Stitch, B., 'Faxfleet 'B', a Romano-British site near Broomfleet', *Humberside Perspectives* (Hull University Press, 1990) p. 158–168

Tacitus, *The Annals of Imperial Rome* (Penguin Books Ltd., London, 1956)

Varley, Raymond, *'The Day Castle Hill (Almondbury) Burned Down'*, Yorkshire Journal No. 36 (Smith Settle Ltd., Ottley, 2001) p. 64–68

Vickers, Kenneth, *England in the Later Middle Ages* (Methuen & Co. Ltd., London, 1913)

Waite, Alison, *Exploring the Yorkshire Ouse* (Countryside Publications Ltd., 1988)

Welfare, H. and Swan, V., *Roman Camps in England* (HMSO, London, 1995)

Wilson, David, *The Vikings and their Origins* (Thames and Hudson, London, 1970)

Wright, E.V., 'An East Yorkshire Retrospective', *Humberside Perspectives* (Hull University Press, 1990) p. 71–85

Index